Printing Statement:

Due to the very old age and scarcity of this book,
many of the pages may be hard to read due to the
blurring of the original text, possible missing pages,
missing text and other issues beyond our control.

Because this is such an important and rare work, we
believe it is best to reproduce this book regardless of
its original condition.

Thank you for your understanding.

The Symbolic Process
and Its Integration in Children

A Study in Social Psychology

By

JOHN F. MARKEY

Ph.D., Research Professor of Sociology, Experiment Station,
Connecticut Agricultural College

NEW YORK

HARCOURT, BRACE AND COMPANY

LONDON : KEGAN PAUL, TRENCH, TRUBNER & CO., LTD.

1928

Printed in Great Britain by Mackays Ltd., Chatham.

SYMBOLS

" Think of it !   The metaphysician has only the perfected cry of monkeys and dogs with which to construct the system of the world.   That which he calls profound speculation and transcendent method is to put end to end in an arbitrary order the natural sounds which cry out hunger, fear, and love in the primitive forests, and to which were attached little by little the meanings which one believed to be abstract, when they were only crude.

" Do not fear that the succession of small cries, feeble and stifled, which compose a book of philosophy, will teach us so much regarding the universe that we can live in it no longer."

—ANATOLE FRANCE, *Jardin d'Epicure.*

THE SYMBOLIC PROCESS

" No one discovers a new world without forsaking an old one ; and no one discovers a new world who exacts guarantee in advance for what it shall be, or who puts the act of discovery under bonds with respect to what the new world shall do to him when it comes into vision."

—JOHN DEWEY, *Experience and Nature.*

CONTENTS

vii

PREFACE

ATTEMPTS to locate the origin of the symbolic process and
" thinking " in the separate individual are bound to make
them appear an enigmatic gift. But most of those who
endeavour to make such explanations have little hesitation
in assuming that, if the search be long and careful enough,
such phenomena will be located in hidden sources somewhere inside the organism—perhaps cotton-packed to
prevent injury. Man, with such special gifts as these
descriptions would indicate, is liable, for this reason, to be
seen as something separate and apart, unrelated to the
rest of the animal world. *Cogito, ergo sum*—I think,
therefore I am—is a statement so enticing and self-satisfy-
ing, why disturb one's peace at the centre of the universe ?

Scientific advance bids fair to dislocate such ideas and
to emphasize interdependent and social characteristics.
But, judged by the tenacity with which it sticks, the conception of the self-sufficing and socially independent
individual must belong to a collection of embalmed ideas
which missed disintegration at the appropriate time.

The recent Gestalt theorists, in spite of their brilliant
work, have gone in regard to the problem under consideration little beyond pointing out mysteries which
require explanation, their next and more difficult task—a
task which greater attention to social interrelations will
facilitate. Recent behaviouristic explanations have also
suffered from ignoring important social factors, which, if
cognizance were taken of them, would have furnished a
very effective defence for the behaviouristic position, but
which, when ignored, have left such explanations open to
attack at their weakest point. But theories do not stay
as hot as they are baked ; cooler analysis discloses the

parts not well done. Considerably more must come off the scientific griddle before intellectual nourishment is properly taken care of on these points.

When adequate attention is given to the social relations and interactions involved in the symbolic process, much of this mystery is cleared up. Man is seen to be one with the other animals, the differences being of degree rather than of kind. The behaviouristic position becomes a tenable one in the field of " mental " phenomena without either positing a body-mind dualism or ignoring facts of human experience.

The main task of this book is an explanation of the social processes in the genesis, integration, and functioning of symbols. There is an obvious need for such a systematic treatment, and a clearer statement of these processes.

It might be of interest to note that this study was preliminary to a project in delayed reaction experiments with children during the period of language beginnings, which was outlined in connection with the Child Welfare Institute at the University of Minnesota. Due to the limits of time and the lack of an adequately accessible group of children at the proper ages, this interesting sequel was not immediately practical.

In describing the complex process of symbolic integration, it was convenient to use some short-hand terms—mnemic, engrams and engramic—which may not be familiar to everyone. These were used to indicate the large complex mass of physiological or material changes which remain as a result of excitation or stimulus response behaviour and which later may be re-aroused or re-activated upon proper stimulation. There is involved here a large number of residual and auxiliary responses which occur in association with subsequent stimulation. If these short-cut terms mean something different from this to some readers, or, if they prefer the more elaborate statement, the above content may be substituted for them.

One of the methodological principles employed deserves special mention. The results from its use seem to justify its wider application in sociological study. It is based upon a definition of *social* which is broad enough to include influences in all organic groupings. It is the comparative examination of other animal groupings for social phenomena similar to those occurring in human groups.

The analysis of speech behaviour also adds weight to another principle which is often not recognized clearly. This is that speech reactions are to be analysed according to the function which they perform in social behaviour. The face value of the particular words used is not so important as their response relation to the stimulus situation. Some responses to questionnaires, for instance, are nothing but attempts to create a favourable impression and not an effort to give accurate responses to particular questions. Speech reactions require a behaviouristic analysis, and by the use of the behaviouristic method reflective behaviour (thinking) and the symbolic process are actually observable and analysable. In reality the observation of reflective behaviour is an every-day occurrence.

Those who do not wish to go into the historical trend may read Chapter II at places which appear suggestive to them, or may go immediately from Chapter I to Chapter III without destroying the unitary character of the treatment.

The endeavour of Ogden and Richards to formulate a science of symbolism (in *The Meaning of Meaning*) is a stimulating and suggestive piece of work which all those who desire a clearer understanding of communication should read carefully.

Previous to the present work, my study under the stimulus of Professor Ellsworth Faris in social psychology gave me an orientation in that field which has been of great value in carrying on this research. The pioneering work of Professor K. S. Lashley in the behaviouristic field, his instruction and that of Professor R. M. Elliott have also had their direct influence upon this investigation. The first part of it, more particularly the historical part embodied in Chapter II, was begun under the much-appreciated encouragement of Professor L. L. Bernard, with his interest in what he has termed the psychosocial environment.

There are other precursors too numerous to mention to whom it would be a pleasure to give acknowledgment, but in connection with this study these four seem to be especially deserving of mention, with the addition of another, Mr. William H. Markey, whose searching mind and intellectual freedom has had a general and specific influence hard to measure.

In the course of the book, reference gives acknowledgment to particular sources. Of these, Mead and Dewey are of especial importance and should by all means be read by those interested. I wish to thank Miss Marion Mattson, who made available to me an unpublished manuscript, in which she had treated data collected at the Merril-Palmer school in Detroit.

Throughout the book I have had the penetrating suggestions and criticisms of Professor Dorothy P. Gary, to whom I wish to express my especial appreciation for her interest and help.

I wish also to indicate my appreciation for the helpful suggestions particularly of Professors F. S. Chapin and C. R. Bird and to thank for their comments Professors W. S. Miller, P. Sorokin and D. F. Swenson, all of whom have read parts of the manuscript.

If this study adds to the understanding of social life and stimulates to further investigation, two of its objects will be realized.

J.F.M.

Minneapolis, Minn.

CHAPTER I

THE sage who said, " Scratch a savant and find a Tartar," would make us all out as wild men. No one has ever sifted the grains of truth from the saying—it would perhaps not be worth while. But it does express the fact that all are subject to irritant influences which exert a profound effect. And when people are seen to be not such mythical beings, each encased within his varnish-coat of social veneer, but social groupings and social beings—interpenetrating systems of interaction which does not stop at the surface, the predicament is a real one.

The scratching is that of social interaction itself, which goes to the core, frequently moulding persons or groups into comic, or more often, tortuous shapes. To eliminate this may require a major operation. The extraction of undesired social interrelations is not similar to throwing off a cloak, but resembles taking steam from water, or moisture from the human body—a consuming process. In any case, it is a precarious undertaking. Although often unsure of what they really want, groups of persons are sure that they get and have a great deal of warped and undesired social life. So that, from one angle or another, everyone wishes to control the persons, groups, or processes involved, either to get more of what is wanted or less of what is not wanted. This is just a way of saying that social control, involving more accurate knowledge, is a pressing problem. The problem is to a large degree responsible for the development of the social sciences, and is destined to be a much more potent stimulus as social relations become more complex.

In its largest sense, social control may be thought of as all the influences which act and react in social groups, as well as the influences exerted by the group upon its surroundings. Such a usage makes it practically synonymous with social influences of all sorts. It comes to mean simply the social interdependence, in a mechanistic and mathematical sense, of social interaction. As such it loses its distinctive characteristics, being diluted and attenuated to include all of social phenomena.

There is another and more limited idea of social control, *i.e.*, those social influences and social changes which are a function of the formulated plans, objectives, or sanctions of the group. Whatever may be the means used, it is the manipulation of the social processes themselves which is the significant part of social control. It is the behaviour process of utilizing social influences whereby the group (or individual) attempts to realize some objective.

Unless social groups are able to set up such objectives which they find desirable and then bring the proper mechanisms into operation to obtain these ends, they can hardly be said to have " controlled " the social processes in any real sense.[1] That is, some sort of reflective behaviour or " thought " activity must be involved.

There is no " uncaused " factor called for in this connection. It is not done by magic—at least this study is not proceeding upon such an assumption. It merely means that groups and individuals plan, more or less clearly, and then work to realize these plans. In a similar manner we control physical laws in order to run automobiles, build skyscrapers, and fly aeroplanes.

In such a conception of social control this " looking ahead," " planning," and " selecting " takes on major importance. Here it is that accumulated knowledge and

[1] If any one has an animistic idea of ends, that the end somehow inserts itself at the beginning in any other manner than the sequential order of events, he might find it instructive to read Dewey (1925, Ch. III).

particularly the social sciences may be utilized. What is the nature of socially reflective " thought " which is thus a prerequisite and a part of social control ? The reflective or ideational process, which for purposes of approach we have designated the symbolic process, has furnished the basis for this study ; a sociological research in the symbolic process and its integration in children. It is assumed that a study of the origin and nature of words, signs, symbols, including significant objects and symbols in art, ideas—the symbolic process—will throw light on the mechanisms used for social control.

The first task is a brief survey of the conception among representative American sociologists of the origin and nature of the symbolic process.

The second is a critical analysis of the process in the light of psychological and sociological experiment and investigation and material gathered from child study. The main avenue of approach will be through a study of the integration of language symbols.

The third task will be to draw some implications of the process, for social control.

Those who prefer more structuralistic terminology would use environment for a great deal of what is included above under the term process.

CHAPTER II

The Trends

THE main lines of thought may be summarized in the trend from an individualistic subjective structural conception to a social objective behaviouristic conception. The whole movement stands out clearly, although it is difficult to point out many sociologists who hold one of the views completely. Most of them represent transitional stages in one or more of the aspects involved.

The Individualistic Subjective Structural Conception

The individualistic subjective structural conception of social interaction and the symbolic process is as follows : Mind and ideas are primarily individual facts and only secondarily, if at all, social facts. This ready-made individual, to a great degree socially independent, is much of a separate unit, quite complete in himself. The symbolic process, in so far as it is thought, ideas— " psychic "—is also subjective. The symbolic process, when it consists of spoken words, visible signs, etc., is objective, but these signs and symbols are arbitrary, merely superficialities ; the real thing is the subjective individual process.

Usually, according to this conception, social groups are made up of but little more than the " sum of " such individuals. These atoms and their relations, which are relatively external to the individuals, make up the structure of social life. Thus it appears as a static framework by which social activities are carried on. The

4

structures within the individuals are mind, ideas, thoughts. Dewey's suggestion that an interdict be placed for a generation upon the use of such words as mind, matter and consciousness as nouns, obliging us to employ adjectives and adverbs, mental and mentally, etc. (1925, p. 75), would be somewhat abhorrent to those who conceive of the individuals' grand possessions as *a* mind and *some* thoughts. It would possibly not be so serious for the next generation. By the phrase *a* mind and *some* thoughts, the purpose is not to imply that these do not exist as much as trees or lakes exist. The point being emphasized is the difference between looking at thoughts as little structures stored in the mind and seeing thoughts as actions, as responses.

The background of earlier sociologists was permeated, as a rule, with the individualistic structural psychology. Psychological thought had not escaped from metaphysical solipsism, nor has it yet escaped, except in a small degree. Considering the period in which these early writers lived who represent most clearly this conception, they are to be commended for what they did see accurately rather than censured for what they saw inaccurately. One influence from which they did not escape was the individualistic refraction of that time.

The clearest examples of the individualistic subjective structural conception are Ward, Ross, and, to a lesser degree, Giddings.

Ward was perhaps the most consistent in his individualistic interpretations. The mind and intellect existed before the group. He speaks of early mankind being without society (1910, II, p. 229, 221 ; I, p. 451, 461). For Ward there is no question—the egg produced the hen —human association was the result of the " perceived advantage " which association yields, and it came into existence " only in proportion " as that advantage was perceived by the intellect. Thought and reason went

B

before, and produced every institution in society (1898 a, p. 91; b, p. 183; 1906, p. 63). The mind is the source of the social forces.

He treats the mind as an entity,[1] although he attacks this idea as a most serious obstacle to psychological progress. This objection seems to have been a sleight-of-hand performance through which his scientific ' conscience ' was satisfied. He was a monist with matter as the basic assumption, consequently mind must be a relation of matter (1893, p. 225 f; 1906, p. 89 ; 1910, I, p. 408 ff). But certainly, in his treatment, the individual has *a* mind and *some* thoughts. Agreeing with Locke, he says that the mind " without experience " is a blank sheet of paper or an empty cabinet. All except the very poorest " strawboard intellects (idiots) are capable, like the boxes, however rudely made, of holding any of the things that are put into them and of preserving them securely " (1906, p. 268 ff). The mind is represented by both the box and its contents. The intellect (capacity to acquire knowledge of objects) is " purely psychic " and " not at all of a physiological nature " (1893, p. 225).

Being evolutionary in his point of view, he did think of the mind as an evolutionary development of capacities already existing in the animal world. He states that although the intellect has probably thus far been confined to man, it is only an amplification of the capacity which resides in the lowest organized beings (1906, p. 333 f; 1910, I, p. 384). However, his discussion of reasoning and mental activity in animals is quite intellectualistic.

Achievement and knowledge (all achievement is knowledge) is individual. In the conquest of nature the individual " seems to be everything and society nothing but the beneficiary of all this gain as it leaks through the individuals' hands . . . " (1906, p. 6 ; 1911, pp. 41, 547–555).

Of course, after knowledge has been produced society

[1] Bodenhafer (1920–21) comes to a similar conclusion. He gives a pointed discussion of the individualistic tendencies of Ward, among others, in relation to the group concept.

has a great deal of control over it and the " filling " of the individuals' minds. Thus, "all the geniuses, all the heroes, all the great men of the world " have been products of " the local, the economic, the social or the educational environment " (one or other of the artificial environments) (1906, pp. 269, 293).

Language is a product of the individual's intellect. It is among the earliest of human institutions and was " certainly spontaneous " (1911, p. 188). It was a result of the pressing need of the mind for communication. Thought " was not content simply to struggle for expression." It applied the " indirect method," *ergo*, language (1910, II, p. 180 *ff*) !

Ross is probably as extreme, although not as consistent in his statement of the individualistic nature of the mind and ideas—but consistency is a hard virtue in much more tenable positions.

According to him, the " dialectic " of personal growth by which " the thought of the other person is built into the very foundations of the thought of one's self," is not " strictly speaking " social. His criterion of social is the action of man on man. The dialectic is a preliminary process not strictly involving this kind of action (1919 a, pp. 5, 95–98).

The innovating individual is an extra-social or sub-social factor (1919 a, p. 227 *f*). Inventions, new ideas, etc., are thus individual products, and it is not society that kindles strange longings or invents new pleasure, but " superior individuals " (1920 a, p. 329). The genius is in no wise a social product (1919 b, p. 360—a view in marked contrast to that of Ward. The causes of social phenomena are individual and to be found in the human mind (1920 b, p. 41 ; 1919 a, pp. 152, 198).

In short, Ross regards man's social union as a late advent. He sees a great drama in which this remarkably independent individual duels against social control for individual ascendancy. If the personality is left to freely unfold, it may arrive at a " goodness all its own."   (1920 a, pp. viii, 14 ; 1919 b, p. vii.)

Giddings' conception of the social makes a sharp contrast to that of Ward and Ross.   The individual is not an independent starting point for the social.   Neither the individual nor society are prior to the other.   The study of sociology is extended to include the natural grouping and the collective behaviour of living things, " including human beings " (1922, pp. 101, 225 ; 1920, p. 399).

Regarding ideas and mental development, he is somewhat similar to Ward in that he holds that other animals have ideas and generalize.   But they do not make an abstract idea as such an object of contemplation.   Their generalization and logic is that of recepts, not of concepts. They have language but not speech (1920, p. 222 *ff*). Speech is evidently associated in his mind with concepts and abstract ideas (symbols).   He does not develop the point, however.

He accepts Donovan's theory regarding the social origin of speech.   Donovan's theory is that the festal occasion furnished the conditions for this development.   The association of musical tones with vocal sounds or cries, reproducing a state of emotional excitement pertaining to play or pleasurable action gave the basis for the " fusion " of concepts.   War and phallic dances may become so real and intense as to end in natural passion (1891).

Human nature is also associated with the development of speech.   From the moment that the hominine species began to practise speech, however awkwardly, it began to develop a human nature (1920, p. 225).   The influences which have created the human faculty are mutations " creative of intelligence on the one hand, natural selection and social pressure on the other. . . ."   It is " preeminently " the social nature and is distinguished from the original nature which consists of hereditary mechanisms

(1922, pp. 226 *ff*, 103, 112). However, the original nature is yet quite dominant according to Giddings (1922, p. 291).

Although Giddings finds speech and ideas social in origin, it is quite evident that he misses some of the social factors involved. It is true, he does recognize to some extent the importance of self-stimulation, dramatization, acting and " conversationalized consciousness " (1922), in the development of the individual. But this is without seeing clearly their social nature and relation to the symbolic process.

Only a part of thought or knowledge forms the " social stuff." The social stuff in " so far as it is intellectual " is one kind of knowledge in particular ; namely, knowledge of resemblances, knowledge of those modes of like-mindedness that make co-operation possible (1899, p. 22). The material of society is a plural number of like-minded persons (1922, p. 167).

Here we are brought back sharply to an individualistic conception of ideas and symbols which are contained in the minds of distinctly separate individuals (1922, pp. 154, 167, 256).

Simple like-mindedness may be a very weak tie between persons. There is a part truth in Ross' statement that these unities " do not imply anything in the way of combined action or practical co-operation."

In the light of the preceding, the individualistic structural nature of this conception of "mind," "thought," ideas and symbols should be clear. However, some further explanation of the subjective aspect—the third partner involved—seems necessary.

The problem runs : Thought and ideas are often said to be subjective and unobservable. In this case the symbolic process would certainly be subjective, or, if symbols were limited to visible and audible signs, words, etc., these would merely be an objective shell for the subjective kernel. Again, if one is taking a structural point of view regarding ideas and thoughts as fixed and established, these might also be said by some to be objective as well as the visible and audible symbols. However, few, if any, structuralists would want to admit such objectivity to ideas. Yet with such a structural view the process of thinking, at least a very significant aspect of the symbolic process, would still be subjective and unobservable. A third position may be taken ; namely, that thinking and the symbolic process is objective and observable. In reality there are only the two views to be considered, the first and third. In any dynamic account of real process the second flies to pieces, resolving itself into the other two views.

Ellwood has taken the rôle of apologist for the subjective in social science ; consequently, he may well be taken as an example of this aspect in preference to the writers previously discussed. The individualistic structural aspects are not so pronounced in Ellwood, although his subjectivism tends to bring them into relief. It is perhaps to a considerable degree responsible for them, for Ellwood must also be classed as a social functionalist in spite of his subjective theories.

According to Ellwood's view, social reality is essentially subjective or an " intersubjective " relation. To make sociology purely objective is to deprive it of its essential character (1912, p. viii ; 1925, p. 7 ; 1918, p. vi f).

For Ellwood, the fundamental social fact is co-ordination and co-adaptation of activities of the group (1912, p. 144 ff). These social co-ordinations have their subjective and objective expressions. The subjective expressions are feelings, emotions, ideas, beliefs, social attitudes, social patterns, etc. (1925, pp. 59, 152–156, 192). The objective expressions are folkways, social habits, objective or visible regularities and uniformities, forms and modes of association, institutions, and what is particularly important from our standpoint, signs, symbols, spoken words, etc. (1925, p. 151 f; 1918, pp. 83, 130 f). This classification places signs and symbols in one category and ideas in another.[1]

The basis for subjectivity is the individual. Only the individual's mind is supposed to think and have ideas. The mind is a separate entity within the individual, for there is no direct causal connection between one mind and another (Ellwood, 1918, p. 79 *f*). The social process is the action and reaction of " mind upon mind " through the " intermediation of physical stimuli " (1918, p. 80).

A sharp line is drawn between psychical and physical. The psychical correlates with the physical and neural, but they are distinct (1918, pp. vi *f*, 33, 72, 86). This is a reason for denying the possibility of a mechanistic explanation of social life, because mechanical, evidently used by him in the sense of physical, would exclude the psychical (1918, p. 16).

The danger for the social scientist of such a dualistic conception should be clear. It tends to give two separate worlds with a chasm more or less wide gaping between. The psychic tends to become something inscrutable and arbitrary. Its processes are instrumental but " not in a strictly causal " way. Psychic phenomena are not to be treated in a " causo-mechanical " manner (1916–17, p. 304).

Such a theory leads to a juggling between two frames of reference in which the performer does a sort of tight-rope dance with one end of the rope wabbling in uncaused movements. It is a species of obscurantism, a kind of bulwark to protect vacuous spots in the scientific world.

In his evolutionary approach Ellwood is on much surer ground. He emphasizes the fact that mind and all forms of consciousness have been developed in and through a social life-process as an instrument of association (1918, p. 57 ; 1912, p. 281). Cultural or human evolution is simply due to man's greater intellectual capacity (ability to form abstract ideas, etc.), and his greater capacity to form acquired habits and not an absolutely new factor or

---

[1] Similar classifications with variations may be found in Ross (1919, p. 98), Giddings (1920, p. 146 *f*), and others.

factors which are not found in the animals below man. The type of association has changed, but not the fundamental nature of it. Thus human evolution is a continuation of animal evolution (1918, p. 38 *ff*).

In spite of this evolutionary conception of the development of the mind, thought is so separate in association with others that it is not the content of our social life, or " in any sense the social reality." It is the instrument by which society has secured greater adaptation.

The way in which individualistic and structural conceptions tie into and find a source of support in subjectivism should be quite apparent.

The Social Objective Behaviouristic Conception

Subjectivism ended the section just closed, but it is with us yet. The division of the social process into subjective and objective is at present a common practice among sociologists. The trend toward objectivity has scarcely moved the subjective conception, and sometimes has even served to put it a little more securely under cover to do its work perhaps even more insidiously. Subjective theories have withstood the advances made in the social, the functional and objective understanding of mind, ideas, and thought. At last the behaviouristic psychology has placed dynamite near its heart ; the explosion may destroy something, at least a considerable amount of fear is evidenced, but a sounder foundation for the social sciences may result.

The objective trend is a part of the whole scientific movement. The cultivation of any field of phenomena with the application of the scientific technique brings such a trend inevitably. The accumulation of data and knowledge introduces it to a greater degree. Such a consideration as is given to the social process, the group concept, social interaction and the like, play an important part. As invaluable instruments in the scientific method, mathematics, and particularly statistics, might have been expected to have dislodged a greater portion of the subjective before this. But after all, statistical methods are only one aid to theory and hypotheses which need to be checked and tested. The statistician has been theoretically unequipped and the social theorist has been statistically unequipped for the task. Consequently, the existing statistical methods have not had adequate application to social materials, nor have new techniques been sufficiently developed to handle special sociological problems. To assume that sociology will get far without a well-developed theoretical basis is as unwarranted as to assume that it will get far without quantitative testing, in which statistics is a very important tool. So far the statistician has been able to measure some of the cruder and conditioning processes of social life, such as population movements, biological, business and labour phenomena, etc. But we have few ratios and equations for the correlation of concomitant and sequential association in the behaviour process of social interaction itself. Particularly have the so-called psychic and subjective eluded the statistician.

Behaviourism is a direct attack upon the subjective. As a method, it furnishes theoretical as well as factual ground for a quantative procedure. The behaviouristic approach, now quite respectable and being adopted by sciences depending upon psychological principles, has thus been of considerably more immediate influence in bringing about non-subjective and quantitative analysis. The influence of Pavlov, Bechterew, and the Continental behaviourists along with Watson, Lashley, and the American behaviourists is not to be underestimated. It has shown functionalism a way out of its morass of subjective structuralism. For it is possible for the sociologist to adopt the functional viewpoint and still hold to subjectivism and even structionalism which tends to be a logical end of subjectivism. Ellwood is an example already given of a social functionalist who is still a subjective structuralist.

In order to show a line of development away from a subjective toward a behaviouristic conception of the symbolic process, the following writers will be considered : Baldwin, Bernard, Cooley, Mead, and Dewey. The first three illustrate the functional approach, which is in reality a departure at least in the direction of the behaviouristic, which is directly evidenced in Bernard's work. In this respect as well as in numerous others Bernard should follow Cooley. But for the trend under consideration he succeeds Baldwin in so many ways that the latter might be considered his prototype. Also the functional treatment which is pronounced in Bernard's work apparently has its most unadulterated expression in Cooley. Mead and Dewey illustrate the behaviouristic conception.[1]

The interdependence of the individual and the group, along with the fact that thought is characteristically social, is now generally recognized by sociologists. But the social nature of the symbolic process becomes more and more apparent as the functional and later the behaviouristic conceptions enter into its explanation.

Baldwin associates the beginnings of conceptual or abstract thought with speech and language, silent thought being internal speech (1908, pp. 141–151). Such forms of expression are social, thus thought is the social stuff (1902, pp. 504 ff). This is illustrated in the " dialectic of personal growth," the social give-and-take, in which the senses of self and of others grow up in social terms (1902, p. 13 ff).

To explain this process he uses the theory of imitation. Unfortunately, it does not explain. Imitation is too narrow a concept to contain the social process. And this is more to the point : it is the social process of *learning* and of *interaction* which must be analysed in order to explain the development of the personality and social life,

---

[1] A more extensive summary, including other writers in both of these sections, might have been made ; for instance, including Park, Burgess, Thomas, Faris, Royce, Bogardus, and others who have given attention to various aspects. However valuable this might be, it was not feasible within these limits. The present purpose is to show a main trend of development rather than to give an extended survey of writers.

and to explain the basis for whatever incidental imitation may be involved.

Consequently, while he takes the genetic and functional viewpoint, he gives us little information in regard to the actual genesis of thought and its social origin. As a matter of fact, he states that it is really individual in origin (1902, p. 504). Subjective knowledge is somehow " ejected " (1906 a, pp. 119, 321) by imitation.

To explain the social, the person is referred to ; to explain the person we must go to the group—thus each is taken as given. As a result, one gets through the explanation in the same vicinity from which he started. Ellwood (1901), Dewey (1898) and others have showed so cogently some of the fallacies involved that no more need be added here regarding them and the individualistic and subjective character of Baldwin's theories.

The similarity between Bernard and Baldwin is striking. A large body of his work is also functional, shading off into the structural and subjective in one direction, in the other direction it goes into the behaviouristic.

He also gives a great deal of attention to thought and symbolic content under the term " psycho-social," which he uses in much the same sense[1] as we have been using symbolic process (1926, pp. 76, 80–85).

At a certain stage the symbolic and psycho-social are taken as given (1926, Ch. X). Hints regarding its origin point to the individual. The inner neuro-psychic processes particularly the cortical, seem to be the source of the symbolic process. The " psycho-social " developed in symbolic behaviour (1926, p. 81) and the " symbolic psycho-social controls " originated in " verbal or other neuro-psychic symbolic content in the cortical processes of ourselves and others " (1926, pp. 65, 81). The origins of language and thought go together, internal behaviour being conditioned to symbols by the process of conditioned

[1] Some contradiction exists between the definition and use of neuro-psychic (1924, p. 87), psycho-social and bio-social (1926, p. 81 *ff*), which need not be gone into here. A careful reading will make it evident.

responses. Thus, thinking is a name for symbolic response or substitute internal neural organization (1926, pp. 144–149). This is rather more complete than Baldwin's explanation, although it still lacks in the analysis of the actual social process in which language and thought become what they are.

The subjective nature of the symbolic process is indicated by its connection with an inner psychic something shown in his use of "neuro-psychic," "psychic," "psycho" (1923, 1924, Ch. V ; 1926, pp. 81, 284, 330 *passim*), "neural correlates " (1924, p. 455) and the like. What this psychic is remains unexplained, except that it is connected with the activity of the nervous system and particularly the cortex (1924, p. 87 ; 1926, p. 121). The subjective category is further illustrated by his use of the term itself (1926, pp. 162, 172). Although at one place he makes the significant statement that such uniformities as customs, traditions, mores, public opinion, beliefs, etc., are " as much objective realities as persons, but more abstract realities," he later calls some institutions " primarily subjective," which is " particularly true of morals " ; *i.e.*, the mores (1926, pp. 82 *f*, 542, 580). Also in this connection, conventions, traditions and customs are spoken of as " subjective aspects of institutions." In discussing Ellwood's article on the subjective, Bernard apparently does not take issue with him on the subjective category as such (1919–20).

His treatment of the subjective and psychic does not lead to the conclusion that he regards the psychic as a partially non-causal affair such as Ellwood introduces.

The division between the internal, inner, psychic, and the external, overt, muscular ; between the individual and the environment, and the division between subjective and objective seem to be a species of inner-outer dualism. Apparently at the bottom of his structural tendencies, this tends to make of social life a set of interacting structure rather than an ongoing process. In fact, his exposition of the environmental conception of social life hardly does justice to his conception of its dynamic character (1926, pp. 84, 270). The structural nature of the symbolic process is also illustrated by the concept of the psychosocial environment as being " objectified neuro-psychic behaviour " (1926, p. 83 *f*), an inner content pushed out in some manner, quite similar to the " ejective stage " of Baldwin (1902, p. 14).

The subjective aspect is not to be overestimated. Bernard accepts a behaviouristic position and places emphasis upon the behaviouristic interpretation. But his disclaimer of clarity for using introspective terminology hardly seems sufficient to account for the elaboration of five types of " consciousness " based upon the objects involved, together with another category of " forms of consciousness " (1926, Chs. XI, XII).

Of course it must be recognized that while the use of such words as " consciousness " and " psychic " may keep one out of " Behaviourism's " heaven, one might still be a behaviourist, providing these terms are not used as explanations. Science is also profane. But it is difficult for one to employ these expressions frequently and not become guilty of, or content with, using them as explanations, instead of using them only as pointers to a more definite description in terms of behaviour. Less is apt to be told by their use than is already known about the thing explained.

Bernard's shift toward the objective and behaviouristic is indicated by his use of internal behaviour processes in various descriptions instead of the so-called psychic. There is evidence of the shift in his *Social Psychology*, where symbolic behaviour begins to take a definite place in his terminology and as a behaviour concept. It was not indexed in *Instinct*.

Bernard makes considerable use of the imitation theory to explain the integration of personality, although not as uncritical a use as Baldwin makes of it. This is at least partially responsible, however, for some sparse places in the analysis of the social process of learning and integration required *before* imitation can occur, or *before* the uniformity called " imitation " appears as a result. Bernard recognizes that such integration must occur (1926, page 277), and does go into some phases instructively.

However, the actual genesis[1] of the symbolic process and its relation to such conceptions as the development of " selves," " persons," and " human nature," receive a remarkably small amount of clarification, although he discusses processes which are useful in an understanding of these phenomena.

In discussing Baldwin and Bernard, another phase of our problem begins to stand out more clearly. This is the question of process and content. As indicated by the treatment so far, an analysis of the process has been uppermost. But this is too simple a statement of the case. There are processes and processes. The more specifically and deeply the content of a process is gone into, the more it is found to consist of processes. Another way of stating this is that we have a process containing in co-relation processes as content—a process of processes. Recognition of this would have clarified at least some sociological work.

The structuralist thinks of some of these processes as structures. The relativity of change does vary greatly. And it is legitimate and necessary to hold things relatively still for purposes of analysis. Yet it must be remembered that our universe is a changing one. The functionalist looks at things from this second point of view. The structuralist sees structures functioning, the functionalist sees structures as themselves functional processes. Thus imitation may satisfy when society is seen as a " cake of custom," or as uniform results, but not when society is seen as a process whereby these results are possible.

Keeping the above distinction in mind, we may continue with the development from a functional to a behaviouristic view of the symbolic process.

---

[1] It will be interesting to note whether this genesis is more adequately discussed in his forthcoming book on the social self and personality.

Cooley is a good example of the social functionalist. He cannot be called a behaviourist, although it is probable that a functional explanation gets its clearest statement in terms of behaviour.

According to Cooley's conception, which shows similarity to Baldwin's in this respect, the social process is practically coincident with the symbolic process. Thought and the social are matters of imagination (1902, pp. 56, 60, 100 ; 1920, p. 6). The social self and human nature are imaginary processes and their results.

Such a conception, on its face, is decidedly subjective, even fantastic, particularly if one holds the common view that imagination is unreal and arbitrary. Thus those who explain the social in such terms are apt to be judged or misjudged.

But for Cooley, imagination is " real " and made up of substantial substance, the ongoing organic body of social intercourse in its extended interrelation (1909, p. 61 ; 1920, p. 3 f). Thought is not complete except in social expression, it is " never isolated." Facial expression, vocal tones, symbols and the like are also a part of thought (1902, pp. 32, 56, 81 ; 1909, pp. 3, 61). It involves action as " a part of its very nature."

Thus the elusive process has a tangible basis in interconnected social action and behaviour. If one wishes to look for it, a unification of the subjective and objective may be found in the act, particularly when viewed from such a dynamic conception as that of Cooley regarding the social process. The combination can lead to a behaviouristic viewpoint, but Cooley does not follow to this point. There is even the atmosphere of a disconnected subjective at some places in his writing, as illustrated by the idea that symbols, traditions and institutions are " projected " from the mind (1909, p. 64).

Cooley develops in a very suggestive manner the rise of the social self with the symbolic process. Social interaction and experience, the reflection of the self in the minds and actions of those around—the " looking-glass self "—are the means of its development, not imitation. Cooley makes little use of imitation.   For instance, he does not think that imitation can account for the acquirement by the child of the correct use of the self pronouns to designate itself, nor does a person understand a dog by imitating his bark or facial expression (1902, pp. 71, 158).

Human nature is another phase developing along with the self and thought process (1909, pp. 28–36), based upon a sympathetic understanding between people.   By sympathy he means converse by symbols ; *i.e.*, getting on a common ground and sharing a mental state (1902, p. 102) —" a fusion of persons."

Cooley is on solid ground in his functional emphasis and in his attempt to see the world as a working whole. His little use of imitation along with more definite information about the social contact and interaction which go on in the symbolic process contribute to a more genuine understanding for which he should be given full credit. However, his substitution of and continual reference to imagination in his discussion and description partake of the type going with imitation—descriptions which do not describe.   Thus, in regard to an analysis of the immediate social mechanism whereby thought actually becomes thought and symbols symbolic—it is left to the imagination.   Furthermore, indefinite symbols such as this which are now in process of redintegration make poor tools in scientific analysis.   Nor does his apparent limitation of the social to the human animal ring true on the register of the " world as a whole."

Mead has filled in some of the gaps in the genesis of the symbolic process.   Recently he has also given a behaviouristic account of it.

The development takes place in a social world.   The acting organism by its behaviour " cuts out " of the world objects of immediate experience (1922, p. 158).   For example, food is food on account of the relation and action of the organism to certain substances.   The animal creates its world as truly as does the reverse occur.

Among these objects of immediate experience are social objects because organisms live together in group life. The social act which creates social objects is one which has its occasion or stimulus in the character or conduct of another living organism belonging to the proper group (1925, p. 263). Thus a social object is one that answers to all the parts of the complex act, though these parts are found in the conduct of different individuals (1925, p. 264). The behaviour unit or action sequence may be or become a social object.

The social is not limited to the human animal nor the symbolic process. In such a social world the symbolic process originates with the rise of selves in behaviour, effected by the individual taking the rôle of another in a social act or object (1922, p. 160 ff). This is accomplished by the individual furnishing or producing a stimulus corresponding or answering to the complex act which releases its own response and at the same time releases tendencies to respond as another in the complex social act (1925, p. 265).

From the standpoint of the individual organism, the distance-receptions, use of the hand and other bodily mechanisms, are important in giving a foundation for this activity. However, more immediately associated with it, and helping to make this sort of stimulation possible, are the vocal gesture and the auditory apparatus. The cortex and the central nervous system also provide at least a part of the mechanism which might make this possible by enabling the individual to take these different attitudes in the formation of the act (1925, p. 266).

But according to Mead, if the cortex has become an organ of social conduct making possible the appearance of social objects, " it is because the individual has become a self, that is, an individual who organizes his own responses by the tendencies on the part of others to respond to his act " (1925, p. 267). Thus, while these and other mechanisms are not to be depreciated, the social rôle is

c

of prime importance in the origin of selves and symbols
—a new type of social object.

The vocal gesture or any other act or object which
embodies this characteristic type of social reaction is a
significant symbol. It serves to distinguish the self from
others and to give the meaning of the individual's act in
terms of another's behaviour (1922, p. 161).

The occasion for such symbolic behaviour is an interrupted act or action process in which a definition of the
situation, the stimulus or object involved in further action,
is called for.   It is a continuation of the process by which
individuals create the world and of course are reciprocally
created by it.   In such symbolic behaviour the analysis
takes place in the object while the conflict of responses
takes place in the individual.   " Mind is then a field that
is not confined to the individual, much less located in a
brain." Significance belongs to things in relation to
individuals (1922, p. 163).

The social objects which are thus created are real, and
exist in the same sense as muscles, fearful or attractive
objects, and the like of our so-called physical world.   Nor
can we deny " this sort of objectivity to imagery, because
access to it is confined to the individual in whose world
it is." This does not make it less objective. (1925,
p. 258.)

The manner in which an object becomes subjective
according to Mead is by its being referred by an individual
to his self (1912, 1922, p. 159).

Concerning the adjustment or analysis situation, Mead
has given an earlier account of it under the conception of
the psychical state (1903), a cogent analysis regardless of
some subjective terminology.   Other writers have given
useful treatment of it ; for instance, Thomas and Znaniecki (1909, 1920) a functional rather than a behaviouristic
account.   Dewey develops the conflict conception in this
connection.

Mead and Dewey show the social objective behaviouristic conception of the symbolic process more clearly perhaps than any other writers.   Their work is supplementary.

Dewey is similarly insistent upon the fact that speech and knowledge are social in origin and essence.[1] Ignoration of this fact has made the behaviouristic explanation appear arbitrary.   " Failure expressly to note the implication of the auditor and his further behaviour in a speech reaction is, I think, chiefly responsible for the common belief that there is something arbitrary, conceived in the interest of upholding a behaviouristic theory at all costs, in identifying thought with speech.   For when speech is confined to mere vocal innervation, the heart of knowledge is not there.   But neither is the heart of speech."   (1922 b, p. 565.)   The origin of language is in the social *use* of gestures and cries.   It is a mode of interaction between at least two beings (1925, p. 185).   The object of knowledge or speech is the ultimate *consent* of the two co-ordinated responses of speaker and hearer.   Without this confirmation and correspondence of co-respondents neither speech nor knowledge is present (1922 b, p. 566).

Real speech and knowledge develop and operate in an adjustment situation.   The speech reaction which constitutes knowledge is such because it serves to supplement or complete behaviour which is incomplete or broken without it.   It is " back into " the thing for which it answers (1922 b, p. 563).   Speech is not merely additive, a supernumerary.[2]

The more complex development of the higher animals, particularly the human animal, makes a more complex adjustment necessary and possible.   Simple organisms have an immediate contact-activity.   There is present immediate sensitivity or feeling, but no " knowledge " (1925, p. 256 *ff*).   But the organism, particularly the more complex it is, also responds to these qualities of immediate feeling, so that they become productive of results and hence potentially knowable or significant (1925, p. 269).

[1] At times he unduly identifies social with communication (1916, p. 5 *f.*)
[2] Speech or vocalization for its own sake may show different aspects, but it does not contradict the above.

In higher animals, locomotion, distance-receptions, etc., prolong the break between the beginning and final response. Thus the activities fall into those having preparatory and those having consummatory status. This series forms the immediate material of thought when social communication and discourse supervene. It should be recalled that the series has already developed in interdependent social action. The first term gains the meaning of subsequent activity, and the final term conserves within itself the meaning of the entire preparatory process (1925, p. 270). The organism, then, has an immediate sense of feeling, and having, also through the aid of others, the social mechanism of language, is able to know the other terms of the whole activity. Immediate having *is* and is complete in itself, it is the *using* of symbols for other parts of the action which makes correspondence, meaning, and knowledge (1925, p. 331). Thus immediate having brings the organism into direct contact with experience, feeling, satisfaction, enjoyments, etc., while knowledge serves to enlighten, and vivify by bringing past and present together at this point through the terms of social intercourse upon which knowledge is dependent.

Meaning and knowledge are not, then, something subjective. " Meaning is not indeed a psychic existence ; it is primarily a property of behaviour, and secondarily a property of objects "—a method of action (1925, pp. 179–188). The qualities of organic action ' objectified ' by language are immediate traits of things. This is not " a miraculous ejection from the organism or soul into external things, nor an illusionary attribution of psychical entities to physical things. The qualities never were ' in ' the organism ; they always were qualities of interactions in which both extraorganic things and organisms partake." (1925, pp. 259, 291.)

The case is further illustrated in regard to mind, consciousness and ideas. Mind, according to Dewey, is the whole system of operative meanings. Consciousness in a being with language denotes awareness or perception of meaning, *i.e.*, it is having ideas (1925, pp. 303–8).   It is the intermittent series of here-and-now aspect of mind.   If one goes so far as to ignore the locus of discourse, institutions and social arts and limits the question to the organic individual, the " nervous system is in no sense the ' seat ' of the idea."   The nervous system is the mechanism of the connection and integration of acts. Ideas are qualities of events in all parts of the organic structure, including the glandular and muscular mechanisms, which have ever been implicated in actual situations concerned with extraorganic friends and enemies (1925, p. 292 *f*).   The locus of the mind—the static aspect—are these qualities of action in so far as they have been conditioned by language and its consequences.

The sense in which imagination or consciousness may properly be called subjective is that it involves a dissolution, a redirection, a transitive transformation of objects or meanings in a medium which, since it is beyond the old and not yet in a new one, may be termed subjective (1925, pp. 220, 308), a conception much the same as Mead's (p. 22).   Subjective and objective thus used to distinguish factors in a regulated effort at modifying the environing world do have intelligible meaning (1925, p. 239), and the subjective process has some particular reference to individual behaviour systems.   Different temporal events of social activity are thus brought together.

Such a conception as we see is at variance with the common one regarding the subjective living is an empirical affair, not something which goes on " below the skin surface " of an organism.

A further point regarding perceptive awareness is necessary in order to emphasize the real and objective character of meanings and ideas.   The notion is current that the cognitive perception of a physical object is intrinsically different from the perception of an idea.   This is a fallacy.   " The proposition that the perception of a horse is valid and that a centaur is fanciful or hallucinatory does not denote that there are two modes of awareness, differing intrinsically from each other.   It does, however, denote something with respect to causation . . . the specific causal conditions are ascertained to be different in the two cases " (1925, p. 322). Thus, so-called sense perception is not primary in knowing (1925, pp. 332–339). Knowledge consists of objects, *i.e.*, events with meaning obtained in the social community of intercourse, so that all objects are known in the same manner through overt acts of taking and employing in social interaction. This holds for behaviour objects as well as physical objects. Apart from " considerations of use and history there are no original and inherent differences between valid meanings and meanings occurring in revery, desiring, fearing, remembering, all being *intrinsically* the same in relation to events." This fact is the gist of the condemnation of introspection (1925, p. 339). Introspection assumes a *direct* knowledge of events.

Dewey also gives considerable attention to human nature and the development of the self (1922 a, 1925, Ch. VI) as well as other facts which serve to indicate the content of the symbolic process. For this process is replete with human significance.

CHAPTER III

THE SOCIAL BEHAVIOURISTIC APPROACH—A GENETIC AND COMPARATIVE STUDY

THE increasing importance attributed to social behaviour in the symbolic process has been discussed in the preceding chapter. This approach will be applied to the present analysis. By " social " is meant those influences exerted by organisms of the group upon each other, and those responses which are made to other organisms as a result of these influences. The main task is to analyse the materials in order to see clearly the operation of these social interactions.

The behaviouristic approach has been so well established as a sound methodological principle that its application to this problem is an obvious necessity. This is particularly true on account of the fact that the symbolic process has been held as one of the strongest vantage grounds of introspectionism and subjectivism. However thriving these two institutions may have been at one time, their present bankruptcy certainly gives reason for the trial of other frames of reference.

It is not the intention to enter into a discussion of the metaphysical questions lying behind the behaviouristic method. The assumption is that the universe is manifest to us by its activity and by our behaviour in reference to it. This, of course, does leave the door open for one to posit whatever he may by act of belief or faith wish to hypothecate as lying behind phenomena. But this question is one for philosophy, science can deal only with observable phenomena. Having ruled out the metaphysical question, one may not therewith deny facts of experience, as some have done. The object is to discover how closely the

behaviouristic account will fit and explain the observed
facts. This does not, however, mean that assumptions
merely read into behaviour processes by some recent
psychologists must also be accounted for. By the use of
the behaviouristic method it is not meant to espouse an
" ism," but to adopt a method of studying psychological
phenomena as composed of acts and action on the part of
biological organisms living in the world to which they
respond. Those behaviouristic assumptions which deny
facts which are often called thought, mental, conscious and
the like, are not acceptable. Nor are the assumptions
acceptable which deny that a behaviouristic study of
such phenomena can be made.[1] It is accepted that there
are facts which are designated by such categories and the
problem is to see whether they may be explained by the
behaviour, the action, of physiological organisms. There
is no pretence that such an approach will leave nothing
more to be known. This cannot be said of any science or
method. The attempt is to discover whether such things as
are sometimes termed " mind," " consciousness," " psychic"
and the like which do not appear to be biological structures
can be more completely explained in terms of the behaviour
of organisms than by positing them as separate or special
structures or elements introduced *ex cathedra*. The
attempt is to see how far mind *et al.* may be explained as a
particularly integrated type of behaviour ; *i.e.*, to look
at mind as action.

   For the present purposes, a symbol may be defined as
an act or object which is marked off by behaviour as a
substitute for a stimulus-act or -object and a response-act
or -object, and which is also at the same time set off by
behaviour as different from them. The symbol has a
double validity, that is, for both the stimulus and the
response. The object spoken of is a behaviour object,
one which has received its character as an object due to
behaviour responses—this holds regarding all objects.
In view of this fact, the definition of a symbol may be

   [1] For varieties of behaviourism *see* Woodworth (1924), Lashley (1923,
pp. 238–40), and Ogden (1923).

expressed a little differently as an act which is a stimulus-substitute for another act often not present, and at the same time is a stimulus for a response to—something to be done about—this other act, while the stimulus substitute is also marked off by behaviour as distinct from the other act and the response to it.

While language symbols might be used as practically synonymous with this definition, it would probably be preferable to restrict language to speech and gesture symbols and retain the term symbol to include also other objects, such as emblems, art, etc., which have this particular relation shown in its clearest form in language.

The genetic development of symbolic behaviour will be traced from the standpoint of the individual and of the larger group process.

Behaviour is a continuous process. For purposes of getting a steady look at it, the act and the S-R (Stimulus Response) process furnish points of reference from which uniformities, dependent and sequential correlations may be measured and induced. The S-R relationship or phases of the act being such a generally recognized frame of reference may be accepted as a common ground for departure. It gives a basis for a functional (in the mathematical sense) and mechanistic explanation. Such an attempt to thus establish uniform and interdependent relationship is sound and necessary if we are to have a nomological science of behaviour. Any departure from a S-R (dependent) relation should be critically examined to ascertain the dependent or sequential character of it. Nor is the S-R equation of itself an " object with power," the functional nature is to be shown by scientific procedure, not otherwise assumed or taken for granted. The work of neurologists and psychologists such as Pavlov, Jennings, Sherrington, Loeb, Herrick, *et al.* has already given firm ground for the assumption of such mechanistic relation in behaviour processes.

In studying the development of symbolic behaviour it will be one of the chief tasks to see whether this remains true in this latter field of activity as well.

The development of conditioned reflexes and conditioned responses is also well established upon a physiological basis, particularly due to the work of the Russian school of objective psychology.[1]

Starting for the time with these concepts, we may trace the early development of the child's symbolic behaviour.

The infant begins with gestures, not used in the sense of language gestures, and laryngeal expressions which have an instinctive basis. The equipment is in common with other animals, but more extensive. About the second half-year of life, the period of articulation begins, the babbling and cooing of the child. Such activity is particularly important as a means to the establishment of circular reflexes or responses between the sound of the syllable and the response of speaking it. This is the requisite situation for the establishment of the conditioned response. The vocal motor synaptic resistance is lowered or completely overcome at the same time that the auditory stimulation occurs. From now on articulation may be controlled through the auditory receptor. The child becomes conditioned to the sounds produced by the vocal apparatus of other persons.[2]

The theory so far outlined, as Allport states, is hypothetical, as precise psychological data are lacking. The question lies between two main theories, that of instinctive imitation and that of the conditioned auditory-vocal response as outlined above. Such control by surrounding sounds is what is so often called imitation; the literature on the subject is full of it. The inheritance of such an already established auditory-vocal connection, however, seems to be purely a speculative assumption. There is little or no positive proof for it.

---

[1] *See* the writings of Pavlov (1923, is a short, interesting article in English), Bechterew, Herrick (1926, Ch. III), Cason (1925), Watson, and others.

[2] This theory so far given has already been worked out by Allport (1924, pp. 178–85, footnote p. 185). It is also contained in Smith and Guthrie (1921, p. 132). Watson gives a suggestive treatment (1924, p. 338 *ff*). A similar basis was indicated by the author (1925, pp. 386, 396), the vocal habits being established by conditioned responses to surrounding sounds, including the child's own voice.

The imitation theory, if accepted, must establish the inheritance of an instinctive mechanism set without learning to operate in an imitative manner to the sounds around the child.   Any other position takes the heart out of the theory as an explanation of this period of development.   An individual cannot imitate anything for which he has not already established some mechanism, either inherited or learned.   Hence, if such structure is not inherited, then it is the learning or acquiring of this ability which interests us and which imitation does not explain. If there are instinctive connections already set and established in any workable condition, it is hard to see why children have so much difficulty in "imitating" correctly.   We are thus thrown back upon a maturation theory, which in this case does not appear applicable but even more speculative, or we must admit the process of conditioning similar to that explained above.   If these so-called instinctive connections are so loose that they require conditioning by vocal and auditory stimulation in order to be operative, then reliance must be placed upon these conditioning processes in their actual establishment, the instinctive basis must be supplemented and cannot be used except as a partial explanation.   The fact often given as evidence that a child responds with a similar word to the stimulus word is no proof at all for instinctive imitation, it merely indicates something to be explained.

More accurately, this process seems to be one of the touching-off of previously acquired vocal habits by the auditory stimuli conditioned to them.   The child in this period of development, as far as can be observed, does not imitate the sounds spoken by another, but responds with the sound for which the word by similarity or otherwise is a sufficient stimulus.   To call this "imitation" seems to be an addition of confusion to the situation.   Present-day psychologists are fairly well agreed that the term "imitation" is little more than an inexact term for similarities observed in behaviour.   (Allport, 1924, p. 239; Thorndike, 1920, Ch. VIII.)

On the other hand, there is positive evidence in support

of the establishment of conditioned circular response.   The
following lines of evidence supporting this hypothesis are
reviewed by Allport (1924, p. 185).

1. If vocal responses are circularly fixed, with the sound
   of speaking them serving as a stimulus, we should
   expect that reiteration of the same syllable over and
   over would be a necessary result.   This is supported
   by the facts.

2. Only sounds which have already been pronounced in
   random articulation can be evoked by the speech
   sounds of others, those which have had a chance to
   be circularly fixated as ear-vocal reflexes.   There
   are data to support this ; for instance, " box,"
   " bottle," " bath," " block," and " bye " all were
   reproduced as " ba " (Allport, p. 185).   Similar
   responses occur for other words.

3. There exist in the central nervous system mechanisms
   adequate for the circular fixation of vocal habits,
   leaving out of account the cortex.   The ear-vocal
   connection is direct and immediate.

4. Congenital or early deafness is usually accompanied
   by mutism.   Deaf-mutes are able to articulate in
   the manner of the random infantile period, but
   cannot, without special methods, learn the use of
   spoken language.

While it is true, as he states, that all these points
might be construed to fit the imitation theory, point 2
would be particularly difficult to explain on such a basis.
In addition, the other difficulties in connection with this
theory remain unanswered.   On the other hand, cases of
the establishment of ear-motor reflexes are clearly established (Allport, 1924, p. 183).

The absence of evidence for this type of " instinctive
imitation " along with the positive evidence for the circular
conditioned vocal-auditory response leaves it as the only
tenable theory.   More positive experimental results in
this connection are desirable.

In Allport's discussion he goes on to show how certain

verbalizations which are evoked by others become conditioned to objects and situations. This is illustrated, for instance, in his figure 19, p. 184. Beyond this his explanation is quite unsatisfactory. It merely amounts to saying in substance that symbols involving thought appear, without saying *how* they appear. The whole process, as he explains it, may not involve the true language habit. Put schematically, the situation may be illustrated by Fig. A without the interchange shown there having effectively taken place. This may represent the activity of any animal trained in vocalization without involving true language or symbolic behaviour. It is just at this point that most psychologists, not excluding the behaviourists, leave out essential social factors. For those who merely accept " thought " and " consciousness " this is not serious; they have accepted a mystery already. But for the behaviourist who tries to explain, particularly the " thought " process, through symbolic behaviour the case is a serious one, for, if he assumes such a direct knowledge of objects, as he must unless he brings in these social factors, he is indeed in a dilemma. Either he must deny facts of behaviour operative in so-called thought process, or these processes must be held to be epiphenomenal. Hunter is another notable example showing the almost total neglect of the further social factors. Consequently " thought " is dragged in bodily by its ears. A very few are exceptional in even recognizing the additional social factors, Weiss for instance.

A more explicit statement of these factors is necessary.[1] The V.S. (verbal stimulus) of another person, the mother or nurse, for example, is associated with a general situation containing specific behaviour and objects. It becomes a conditioned stimulus for the child's responses to the specific behaviour or object, and at the same time an adequate stimulus for the child's own V.R. (verbal

---

[1] In this and following discussions, the term " response " as a general category may include all reactions of the organism, including visual, tactual, auditory, the so-called sensory or affector responses, as well as other reactions, such as glandular and muscular reactions. The affector reactions are one kind of response.

response).   This situation results in the child's own V.R.
becoming conditioned to all these factors in a manner
similar to that in which the mother's or nurse's V.S. is
conditioned.   A factor which often facilitates this process
is that the mother or nurse often imitates the child, instead
of the reverse.   The child's V.S. or V.R. thus becomes
substitutive for the stimulus act or object and for his
own bodily process or response.   Any of the factors

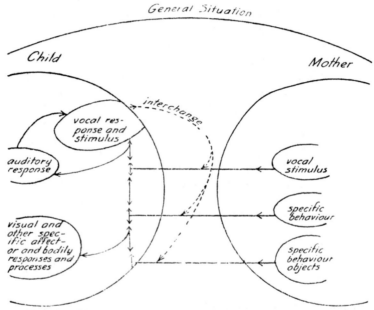

FIG. A.—The responses of the child showing the social interchange
involved in the origin of the true language symbol.   The child takes the
rôle of the mother.

indicated in Fig. A may now serve to call forth the V.R.
of the child.   Another step is required to complete the
true language habit.   When the above conditioning process has gone to the point that the baby's V.R. is effectively
substituted for, or interchanged with, that of the mother or
nurse, we then have the beginning of true symbolic
behaviour.   However, this would not yet be symbolic

behaviour unless the association and conditioning had been carried to the degree that all three of the following factors functioned dependently together. (1) The substitution of the child's V.R. for the V.S. of the other person to such a degree that the child actually performs this act so well that (2) it produces in itself the same tendencies to respond that the other person produced, thus arousing by its own act, as if the other person's V.S. were actually present, the beginning or early implicit or overt bodily responses, to the person or object, which have been conditioned to the person's V.S.   These beginning visual, auditory, motor and other responses being conditioned to, or a stimulus to, behaviour which follows when the original stimulus is present tends to arouse the conditioned or habitual responses of the child.   (3) At the same time, the child also arouses similar and other conditioned responses to its own V.R. on its own validity as a stimulus and as a part of the behaviour processes of the child.   This third factor is facilitated by the fact that the child is used to responding to its own vocal response and also by the fact that the absence or lack of the usual response by the other person inhibits complete expression of the beginning behaviour pattern and tends to direct the behaviour of the child toward its own responses, already in operation, as differentiated from the behaviour stimulus of others.   These reactions of the child which differentiate its own verbal stimulus as being the same or similar to that of the mother and at the same time which give it validity as its own vocal stimulus gives the vocalization the character of a symbol.   These three parts of behaviour merge or integrate into a functional behaviour unit, Fig. A.   We have in this unit the V.S. indicating the absent stimulus and the present response to it.

   Although such writers as Mead, Weiss, and Dewey have not stated the process in the manner given above, their conception of language habits must rest upon some such behaviour process.   Mead's theory of taking the rôle of the other through the use of significant symbols rests directly upon it, the significant symbol having these two references—to the absent stimulus and to the present response (1922). Weiss' theory of interchangeability of receptor-effector mechanisms (1924) is also made clear by this explanation.

The first moment that such an integration occurs in the behaviour of a child must be a startling one. This flash of co-ordination, facilitation, inhibition, summation, and integration of responses which occurs in the behaviour mechanisms would be a novel and extraordinary experience. Of course, it has gradual development in genetic growth.

Helen Keller gives a suggestive description of such a sophisticated — because more artificially induced — analytical integration condensed into a short period of learning.

Such a theory explaining symbolic integration has the weight of psychological and sociological evidence behind it, and provides a basis for a genuine behaviouristic explanation which does not ignore facts of experience. Even though the unsupportable theory of instinctive imitation be accepted, this conditioning process would still be an essential and demonstratable part of language and symbolic development. The period up to the point at which the child's own stimulus is effectively substituted for the other's stimulus has been made fairly clear by various writers. The point which needs further clarification here is this process of social interaction by means of which the child does thus effectively make this interchange. Any act on the part of the child which was conditioned, as described above, in behaviour to the child's own responses and to the other's stimulus and which could be interchanged would probably serve the purpose. As a matter of fact, the process of teaching deaf-muted depends directly upon such a conditioning process. In the life of a normal child the conditioning is built up in verbal mechanisms. These are so similar in the child and the adult that substitution and interchange is bound to occur under the normal conditions of an adult language milieu.

Further, without any previous language there is no

other mechanism or act in the individual's behaviour which would seem adequate to establish the conditioning necessary and be of such a character that the individual could interchange it with some other act or object. Even at this, the process of conditioning would be a precarious one.

The fact that the child does interchange stimuli and takes the rôle of the other person is an observed fact. This has been emphasized especially by Cooley and by Mead specifically. However, there is need for more exact and controlled observation concerning the details of the child's behaviour, especially at the age in which the child is just acquiring symbols. Close observation of this period from the standpoint of these social interactions is a neglected but most important phase of child study, and one which will be amply fruitful of results.

Such data as are available concerning the social factors in symbolic development will be analysed in following chapters. In the next five chapters data regarding the social behaviour involved in symbolic development will be analysed along with materials showing the probable extent of symbolic behaviour in the animal world. Afterward, in Chapter IX, a more thorough analysis of symbolic integration, including these social phenomena, will be attempted. It will then be valuable to relate the symbolic process to so-called thinking in order to see how completely this may be accounted for by symbolic behaviour.

D

CHAPTER IV

FIRST WORDS

It is the third period, the basis for which has been laid by babbling, cooing and random articulation, when the child begins to repeat or attempt to repeat the words of others which concerns us. With this parrot stage already established, the problem is to determine when the true language symbol is integrated.

The data regarding speech development is in the main observational and thus lacks the control which the laboratory gives. The so-called first word is generally listed when a definite vocalization is used to designate a definite act or object. It ought to be clear immediately that such a first word may be wholly on the basis of the conditioned responses as shown in Fig. A, minus the interchange, without involving a true language habit. The attempt of a fond parent to determine the first word used " with meaning " is to be taken with some reservation.

Bateman (1917) has summarized 35 of these " first words" obtained by 28 observers (Table I). The largest group falls at 10 months; 42·85% are in the 10–11 month group, and 74·28% said the first word under 12 months (Table II). The acts or objects indicated by these first words are

14 persons (including two cases where either dady or dog were first) ...	40·0%
18 acts associated with persons (including 3 cases of da for there) ...	51·4%
1 animal	2·9%
(adding the two cases cited above)	(8·6%)
2 mechanical sounds	5·7%
35 Total	100·0%

38

TABLE I.

FIRST WORDS.

SOURCE BATEMAN 1917.

Authority.		Sex.	Time, Months.	Word.	Meaning of Word.	Time of next Word. Months.
English-Speaking Children—						
Bateman	1914	F	10½	Hello		Same time
Bateman	1915	F	10	Daddy		Same time
Bateman	1916	F	11	Bye-bye		Same time
Bohn	1914	F	9	Daddy		Same time
Boyd	1914	F	11	Dada or dog		Same time
Brandenburg	1915	F	10	Bye-bye		12
Darwin	1877	M	12	Mum	Food	Later
Grant	1915	F	12	Bye-bye (?)		Same time
Hall	1896–1897	M	8	Bye-bye		9
Jegi	1900–1901	F	12	Mamma		Same time
Major	1906	M	14	Baby		Same time
Mickens	1897–1898	F	11	Mamma		Same time
Moore	1886	M	10	Papa or Mamma	.	—
Moyer	1911	F	9	Hark		Same time
Nice	1915	F	14	Mamma		—
Pelsma	1910	F	10	Daddy or dog		Same time
Pollock	1878	F	13	Dada		Same time
Shinn	1905	F	10	Da	There	Same time
Total		18				

TABLE I—*continued.*

FIRST WORDS.

SOURCE BATEMAN 1917.

Authority.	Sex.	Time, Months.	Word.	Meaning of Word.	Time of next Word. Months.
German-Speaking Children—					
Ament ...	F	11½	Mam mam	Food	15
Linder ...	F	9½	Papa	Father	Same time
Linder ...	M	13	Da	There	15
Preyer ...	M	11	Hatta	Gone	13
Schneider ...	F	10	Da	There	11½
Schneider ...	F	10	Take take	Dancing	11½
Stern ...	F	9	Ata	Father	15
Stern ...	F	10½	Didda	Tic toc	11
Stern ...	M	11½	Papa	Father	12
Strumpell ...	F	10½	Ssi-ssi	Tea machine	10½
Stumpf ...	M	9½	Papu-papu	Food	12
Togel ...	M	14	O (hoch)	Up	15
Total	12				
Other Languages—					
French:					
Deville ...	F	13½	Papa	Father	Same time
Taine ...	F	10	Wawa	Dog	Same time
Bulgarian:					
Gheorgov ...	M	13½	Dza¹	There¹	Later
Gheorgov ...	M	15	Boc	Up (?)	Later
Polish:					
Altuszewski ...	M	13	Papa	Food	Same time
Total	5				

¹ dza = daj, gib.

TABLE II.

TIME OF USING FIRST WORD.

SOURCE BATEMAN 1917.

Age, months.	8	9	$9\frac{1}{2}$	10	$10\frac{1}{2}$	11	$11\frac{1}{2}$	12	13	$13\frac{1}{2}$	14	15	Total
Number, Children	1	3	2	8	3	4	2	3	3	2	3	1	35

Adding all those pertaining to persons, including the two cases where dog or dady was also used, they comprise 91·4% with only three words falling outside this category —dog, didda for tic toc, ssi-ssi for tea-machine. This is one indication of the rôle of persons and their behaviour in these so-called first words. No doubt parents have facilitated the application to themselves of the sounds which the infant can more readily utter. The prevalence in so many languages of some form of the root ma-ma for mother, pa-pa for father, and other similar derivations strongly suggest this (Buckman 1897, Jespersen 1923, pp. 154–160). The parents and adults are apparently better imitators than the infant.

It is quite a burden upon credulity to accept these words as real language habits. Such words as da for there, didda for tic toc, ssi-ssi for a tea-machine can scarcely be anything but direct responses to stimuli, and not the production of absent stimuli. For instance, it seems quite naïve seriously to maintain that a nine-months-old baby said " hark " with symbolic reference. It is highly questionable whether any out of the whole list can be put in any other category than the parrot talk of infants, not beyond the conditioning shown in Fig. A, minus the interchange. The criterion used for their selection is usually this. The definite association of a name with an object does not of itself indicate real language. However, this does not diminish the fact that these words are associated with persons, which, of course, is to be expected in view of the close association of people with the learning of language. The rôle of persons is further indicated by the fact that if the names for the parents are not the first, they are among the first words. The acquirement of proper names is also significant. But it is a rather curious fact that quite a number of observers exclude proper names in their computations of vocabularies. This is remarkable, even ridiculous, in view of the fact of the association of persons in a child's life. Mrs. K. C. Moore found in her investigation that proper names comprised her child's total vocabulary at one year, and also played an important part thereafter (1896). Among the first words, usually occurring very early, is also a word to designate the child itself, generally the word " baby." As the time of the beginning of true symbolic behaviour is obviously not given in these so-called first words, the question must be deferred until more data are considered.

In the above list of first words even those which are not connected with acting organisms are associated with action in the form of sound. The action content of words will be further indicated in the next chapter.

After the child has once begun to acquire symbolic designations, the process soon becomes rapid and pronounced. The cases upon which a vocabulary count has been kept[1] are generally so lacking in any basis of random sampling that figures given for the total vocabulary at different ages cannot be said to represent the population as a whole for these ages. Consequently, no general curve of learning can be drawn from the figures ; at best they are only approximate. The comparability of one year with another in such data is also questionable, due to varying factors. There is a tendency to notice and report large vocabularies and to overlook smaller ones. Also, probably due to greater convenience, there is apparently a larger number of observations on children in the more educated or well-to-do families, which would tend to select in favour of larger vocabularies. Of course, beginning with the school period, selection obviously enters tending to produce a larger vocabulary figure, especially at certain

[1] See Magni (1919), Doran (1907), Kirkpatrick (1907), and others for summaries ; also cf. Brandenburg (1918), Whipple (1908), Terman (1912, 1915), and Smith (1926) for vocabulary tests.

ages. The averages in Table III, Section A, are given for what they may be worth, and are only suggestive. The vocabularies averaged by Mrs. Nice are taken from different sources, but she makes a practice of deflating for plurals, verb inflections, and the like according to Bateman's rules, so that the figures are thus more representative and more comparable. However, the rapidity of increase is evidently too steep for the general population

TABLE III.

VOCABULARIES.

SECTION A.

Age.	Authority.		No. of Cases.	Average.
1	Bateman	(1917)	35	9½
2	Nice	(1918)	25	508 Probably unduly large
3	Nice	(1917)	11	1338
4	Nice	(1917)	7	1843
5	Nice	(1917)	2	4225 Very large ; probably nearer 2500
6	Nice	(1917)	2	3103

SECTION B.

Smith's test.

Average size of vocabularies.[1]

Age.	Number of Cases.	Number of Words.
—8	13	0
—10	17	1
1—0	52	3
1—3	19	19
1—6	14	22
1—9	14	118
2—0	25	272
2—6	14	446
3—0	20	896
3—6	26	1222
4—0	26	1540
4—6	32	1870
5—0	20	2072
5—6	27	2289
6—0	9	2562

[1] (1926)—figures for less than two years, from lists from mothers.

TABLE III—*continued.*
Kirkpatrick's test.[1]

Grade.	Average.
II	4480
III	6620
IV	7020
V	7860
VI	8700
VII	10660
VIII	12000
IX	13400
Frosh. H.S.	15640
Soph. H.S.	16020
Junior H.S.	17600
Senior H.S.	18720
Normal Sch.	19000
College	20120
Graduate students	20000 to 100000 est.

Brandenberg's test.[2]

Grade.	Number of Cases.	Average.
II	22	4000
III	78	5429
IV	228	6887
V	245	8207
VI	378	9613
VII	300	11445
VIII	255	12819
IX	72	13504
X	71	15340
XI	71	13974
XII	41	14975

for these ages. Observations have it that girls begin to talk somewhat earlier than boys and keep ahead of them in later development as well (Stern, 1924, p. 143). If this is true, Bateman's average for one-year-olds is probably high, as about two-thirds of them are girls. Gesell (1925, p. 217) says that the median 12-months-old child has at least three or four distinguishable words.

[1] (1907)—Based upon sampling from dictionary, estimates obtained from among 2,000 answers of schoolchildren mainly in Massachusetts cities, and upon Bryn Mawr, Smith, Columbia, Brown, Pratt Institute.

[2] (1918)—From 2,000 pupils in 16 schools in Wis., Mo., Colo., from towns of 1200–30000.

Nice (1918) gives as standards of early speech development the following : the first word by 15 months, 200
words and the sentence by 2 years, 600 words and all parts
of speech by 3 years. Besides the figures obtained by
directly counting vocabularies, those obtained by vocabulary tests are also significant and give probably a more
accurate basis for purposes of comparison on account of the
fact that the tests have been standardized and used upon
larger numbers of children. Some of the figures obtained
by vocabulary tests are also given in Table III, Section
B. Whipple's (1908) study in general corroborates the
figures of Kirkpatrick and Brandenburg. Terman's
figures (1912, not included here) are lower, but are perhaps
not so comparable with the other figures, due to the method
of selecting the test words. They were selected from a
smaller total (18,000 vest pocket words) and with reference to the more commonly used words. It is possible
that although his test is a good battery test for intelligence
scoring, it may still not test the total vocabulary range.

There is a great amount of individual and group variation. For instance, Paola Lambroso (Chamberlain 1904)
found in a study that 50 children belonging to the well-to-
do and educated families had much larger vocabularies
than 100 children of poor families. Both in the precocity
with which they interpreted the words and the exactness
reached the children of the former families exceeded
those of the poor in the proportion of 2 : 1. She concludes that the question is not one of defect of intelligence,
but of differing situations. Drevers (1919) in a study of
Edinburgh Free Kindergarten children, coming from one
of the poorest localities in Edinburgh, gives the following
averages taken from a sample which he tried to make
representative :

4 children about 3 years averaged 376 words.
5 ,, ,, 4 ,, ,, 451 ,,
12 ,, ,, 5 ,, ,, 580 ,,

Some of these Kindergarten cases, according to Drevers,
were not mentally normal. Due to the small amount of

time spent in observation in at least four cases, these averages for the children are a little low, the three and four year averages probably being the most unreliable. Based upon similar methods of observation and other data, he estimates as a normal vocabulary from 1,000 to 2,000 words for a child of five years in good social circumstances. Allowance for an underestimation of the poorer vocabularies would still leave a substantial difference. Alice Decoeudres has worked out a language measure for young children and has used it for the ages $2\frac{1}{2}$ to $7\frac{1}{2}$. The results show the language acquirement of the working-class children to be below that of the children of educated classes. Stern (1926, p. 176) calculates from her figures for the two groups that, on the average, the children of the educated classes are eight months ahead of the working-class children of the same age ($2\frac{1}{2}$—$7\frac{1}{2}$). Social influences obviously create individual differences and there are also structural characteristics both inherited and acquired which may influence speech behaviour.

The number of words in common among the children of even the same family may be relatively small. Gale (1900) found among three children of the same family, each vocabulary taken at $2\frac{1}{2}$ years of age, that out of 2,170 words, only 489, or 22·5%, were in common. The two younger children had only 16% in common. Holdren's two children had 40% in common (Gale 1900). Drevers found among the above Free Kindergarten children that the common words were as follows (I have computed and include only percentages based upon the total vocabulary, 2,116 words for the 21 children) :

19 subjects had 2% of the total words in common.
15 ,, ,, 7% ,, ,, ,, ,, ,, ,,
10 ,, ,, 16% ,, ,, ,, ,, ,, ,,
3 ,, ,, 52% ,, ,, ,, ,, ,, ,,

Thirty-three per cent. of the total words appeared in only one vocabulary, not being in common. Drevers considers that the fundamental words in the vocabulary of this type of child may be reckoned under the conditions of the investigation, as all words given by 75% of the children. The 15 cases would probably be a high 75% due to the four short observations. These had only 7%, or 148 words in common out of a total of 2,116 words. These facts indicate some of the wide diversities which may enter into the individual learning curves, of which some examples are given in Chapter VI.

CHAPTER V

THE BEHAVIOUR CONTENT OF SYMBOLS

At this point it will be well to summarize some further facts regarding the action content of symbols. The basis for such a consideration has already been discussed in Chapter III.

There is general agreement among sociological and psychological students upon the fact that symbols are acquired in social interaction. There is also a general consensus that the content of symbols is to a large degree action pertaining particularly to that for which the symbol is a substitute. But there is no agreement that the most complete explanation of symbols is action of one kind or another, or that symbols become what they are through action and are maintained by behaviour processes. A large number of persons wish to posit something over and above this action content, a "meaning" or "consciousness," or some other such factor in addition to behaviour. This problem of knowledge and meaning and the question as to how far the behaviour of organisms will account for meaning will be discussed later. For the present it seems desirable to consider the action content without going directly into this particular problem. However, it might be well to suggest, in passing, something of what is meant by the proposition that meaning exists through action on our part. Take the object " window-glass " for example. Because we can see through it, it is clear ; by touching, feeling and breaking, it is known to be hard ; by acts of rubbing, it is known to be smooth, and so on. Of course, these things are apparently not " known " in a reflective sense until symbols have arisen in social behaviour, thus making it possible for absent and past parts of behaviour and experience to be brought into the present behaviour in an indirect manner by means of these social agencies, *i.e.*, by symbolic action.

The present inquiry will naturally have implications concerning meaning and will also show at least some kind of " meaning " content. It may be added that by the content of a symbol is meant the factors or processes embodied in it which go to characterize it as a symbol and make it more than a mere puff of wind through the vocal apparatus.

The behaviour content has been indicated quite definitely by various social psychologists and psychologists, particularly the behaviourists, who have studied the acquirement of speech in children ; for example, Watson, Allport, Mead, Block, and others. The rôle of action is clearly shown in the child's mastery of the use of symbols in his adjustment to his social surroundings.

In view of its evident importance one might expect that those studies dealing particularly with vocabulary acquirement in children would give a considerable amount of attention to the behaviour content, but he would be generally disappointed. These studies are often given over to a mere tabulation of words and to grammatical considerations rather than to psychological study. By thus ignoring the psychological factors much of this work remains of little worth, even from a grammatical standpoint, in showing the true character of child speech. Most of the studies on the learning of symbols by children classify words into the traditional adult parts of speech. Such a classification may mean very little regarding the significance of these words in the behaviour of the child. It is rather remarkable that during the considerable period in which this phase of child study has been in vogue, so much time has been put upon such comparatively uninformative facts, and little or no attention given to more significant factors. However, sufficient materials have been collected to show some of the importance of action and which yield, by further analysis, valuable information concerning the action content of the child's symbolic behaviour.

The young child has few, if any, words of an abstract nature. Its early symbols are for simple concrete designations of the more obvious acts and action-objects[1] of its surroundings. This has been clearly demonstrated by such investigators as Nice (1917), Boyd (1914), Bohn (1914) and Drevers (1915, III), to mention a few. In addition to this, numerous investigators such as Chamberlain, Tracy, Dewey, Binet, and others have shown that the child's symbols are action words, *i.e.*, their content is action. There is also practically universal agreement upon the fact that the first symbols of the child are in reality word-sentences designating action and object or subject, or all three at once. Thus, for instance, Koffka (1924, p. 301) says a " mother " is not only something which " is so," but more exactly something which " does this," " assists thus," or " punishes so." The gesture language of the child is also a potent testimony of the action content of symbols.

Binet (1890) made a study of his two daughters in an attempt to discover children's interests by asking them the meaning of 33 nouns that he had selected.[2] The selection is somewhat arbitrary, and the criticism might be brought that they lend themselves to the results. However, as the list really appears fairly representative, it is more than probable that any other list would give similar results. Still, if the above criticisms were true, it would not diminish to any appreciable extent the comparative value obtained by using the same set of words with other children and at different ages. This has been done by Barnes (1896–7) ; also by Shaw (1896).

It should also be pointed out that these studies are not studies in introspection ; the analysis is of the responses themselves as such. It might be objected that we are dealing with mere speech reactions and these children may have " meant " something different from what they said.

---

[1] By an action-object it is meant to indicate that our objects exist for us due to behaviour regarding them.

[2] The list is as follows : knife, bread, doll, water, armchair, hat, garden, piece of sugar, thread, horse, table, mamma, potatoes, bottle, flower, snail, mouth, lamp, bird, dog, carriage, pencil, earthworm, shoes, finger, clock, house, wolf, omnibus, balloon, village, box, handkerchief.

This objection is not valid. It is the speech reaction—the naïve response of the child—in which we are interested and from which significant conclusions can be drawn. It is assumed that the child is not outside our universe of discourse ; that when he responds, " A hat is to put on your head," this speech reaction is related to the stimulus word and consequently constitutes one valid indication of its stimulus character for the child.

It is quite probable, too, that the child means his response. Furthermore, a certain " correct understanding " of the stimulus word is not essential ; all that is necessary is some distinctive response to it as a symbol.

Binet's conclusions were that children are impressed to a very small extent by visible aspects of things. Their ideas possess only slight abstract characteristics. Their greatest interest is to be found in the use of things.

This last conclusion is the one which bears most directly upon the present problem. If true, it means that the content of the symbolic process as indicated by the child's defining responses in its early years at least has to do primarily with action, the content of symbols being behaviour or action of one kind or another. Barnes took the same list of words and obtained responses from more than 2000 children in Monterey County, California. Out of these 2000 he took the responses of 50 boys and 50 girls for each age from 6 to 15 years, making 100 for each age and 1,000 in all. The selection was made by taking the first reports which were sent in until each 50 had been selected. It seems that such a selection of responses would be a fairly random one, as far as the action content of responses is concerned. Apparently, such factors as promptness on the part of the teacher had little constant relation if any to the action content of the responses of the children. Barnes classified the replies into 9 categories. Due to the fact that some answers fell under more than one category, the total statements collated were 37,136. An example of a statement falling under several heads is : A knife is a tool (larger term) made of iron (substance) having a blade and handle (structure), and is used to cut bread (use).[1] The question asked was, " What is a . . . ?"

The results of this study are unmistakable regarding the behaviour content of these words. Two of his categories obviously express behaviour, *i.e.*, use and action. The percentages are given in Table IV. The obvious action content is very marked in the earlier ages and decreases with age, at 6 years 82%, at 15 years 33%, almost 50% difference.

As a partial check upon this evidence of action predominance, I classified the responses which Binet records for his children to the same list of words with the exception that with the younger child these words were omitted : clock, doll, omnibus, armchair, bottle, finger. The following words were submitted : papa, spoon, bed, chair, lobster, eye. Responses to several other lists of nouns were obtainable from different sources. These were classified in a similar manner. The results are given in Table V and corroborate the study of Barnes.

In addition to the above, three other sets of data may be given. Chamberlain (1909) gives a list of 1186 words, the meaning of which was asked of a child during its 47th and 48th months. These were taken from the different parts of speech. Checking over these, I found as a fairly conservative figure approximately 70% of the responses expressing obvious action. A stricter consideration of the words should raise the percentage. Wolff (1897) states that in the Boy's Dictionary (the boy was 7 years old) 75% of the less abstract words (not nouns) express action. In the sample facsimile given by her, of 173 words at least 60% indicate action. Shaw (1896) by simple association, no attempt being made otherwise to get the content of the word itself, found for 600 city children between 8 and 13 years inclusive, that 34% of the statements express

---

[1] Examples of other categories :
Action—a clock goes tick-tock.   Colour—a clock is yellow.
Quality—a clock is pretty.   Form—a clock is round.
Place—a clock is on the wall.

obvious action (use or action). He used Binet's list of
words.

TABLE IV.

RESPONSES OF CHILDREN TO NOUN STIMULUS WORDS (ORIGINAL
FIGURES FROM WHICH PERCENTAGES WERE OBTAINED TAKEN
FROM BARNES 1896–97).

Age.	Use and Action.	Larger Term.	Substance.	Structure.	Form.	Place.	Quality.	Colour.	Unclassified.	Total.
6	82·0	3·1	1·8	1·1	·3	·3	1·8	·6	9·0	100·0
7	70·8	7·5	2·4	1·4	1·1	1·4	2·7	1·5	11·1	99·9
8	73·4	6·7	4·3	1·9	1·0	2·8	3·8	·5	5·6	100·0
9	67·8	11·8	6·2	2·6	1·0	2·7	3·0	·8	4·1	100·0
10	61·6	12·1	7·3	3·2	·9	4·3	2·0	·3	8·3	100·0
11	48·3	19·6	10·1	3·9	1·9	5·3	6·3	·5	4·0	99·9
12	46·7	16·6	10·9	5·6	1·5	5·7	4·2	·2	8·6	100·0
13	37·2	22·8	11·6	7·0	3·1	5·5	6·4	·3	6·1	100·0
14	41·2	25·5	9·7	7·6	2·6	4·8	4·6	·7	3·3	100·0
15	32·7	38·0	11·0	6·4	3·1	3·6	3·0	·5	1·8	100·1
Ave.	56·2	16·4	7·5	4·1	1·65	3·6	3·8	·6	6·2	999·9

TABLE V.

USE AND ACTION RESPONSES.

Author.	Child.	Age.	No. of Stimulus Words.	% of Use and Action Responses.
Binet ... 1890	Girl younger	2½—3½	33	87
Nice ... 1917	Girl E	3	14	87
Nice ... 1917	Girl D	4	6[1]	100
Pelsma 1910	Girl E	4	66	78
Binet ... 1890	Girl older	4½—5	33	84

In view of the apparent representative character of
Barnes' cases, although they were from the country, they
are corroborated by Shaw's cases from city children[2] as
well as by the other incidental data cited above, it is
probably that they depict a general situation. The per
cent. of obvious action in the definition at 15 years is
practically the same as that given by Webster for these
words.

[1] One word, bathe, not a noun.
[2] *See* page 59 *ff* for further analysis of Shaw's data.

E

In so far as these data are concerned Binet's conclusions are substantiated, that young children are
impressed very little with abstract characteristics, and are
mainly concerned with use. The term action should be
included because the use of a thing includes action. The
small per cent. of responses in those categories which
approach abstract characteristics is shown in the Table
(IV). Binet's conclusion regarding the small impression
by visual aspects is probably only superficially true and
then only for certain aspects, for the visual function seems
quite important in use and action discrimination.

There is another significant conclusion which may be
tentatively drawn. It is that with increasing age there
is a decrease in *obvious* action content and an *increase* in
refined action content, as shown by such responses as
larger term, structure, substance, and the like (Graph I).
It is undoubtedly true that this trend is not so much a
function of age as it is a function of social behaviour and
experience.

What is the significance of these facts regarding the
action content as indicated by responses to noun stimulus
words, for the content of the whole vocabulary of the child?
If they can be taken to represent only the action content
of nouns in the child's vocabulary this is important, for
the percentage of nouns sometimes goes well over 80%
(see Nice, Boyd, Tracy, and others). Kirkpatrick (1891)
estimates from 55% to 85% nouns. Nouns thus form a
considerable portion of the total vocabulary.

However, the classification of a child's vocabulary upon
the basis of the adult parts of speech is a highly arbitrary
and fictitious process, particularly with reference to
nouns. These first so-called nouns, as Dewey (1894) and
others have pointed out, are in reality verbal-adjectival-
nominal or nominal-adjectival-verbal symbols and the
like. In reality they are action words and word-sentences,
as we have seen, and are often accompanied by the appropriate action on the part of the child. Due to all these
facts it would seem as appropriate to classify the child's
nouns on the basis of usage, as action words or verbs.

Graph 1. Showing the decrease
in obvious Action associated with
the tentatively assumed increase
in refined behaviour
        Analysis of Symbols

Obvious Action
Responses

Use and Action

Refined Action
Responses

Larger   Term

Substance

Structure

Years

Source Table IV

Assuming that these facts are sufficient to indicate the behaviouristic character of nominal symbols, it remains to consider the other parts of speech. Here the task is relatively simpler. Verbs are action words by definition. Adjectives and adverbs, which are of later development, are modifiers, consequently serve to indicate characteristics of other action words. The connectives, forming only a small per cent., serve as aids to other parts of speech and to sentence differentiation. Interjections, also a small per cent., serve as emotional expression. The pronouns stand for nouns, or persons, which are acting organisms. The behaviouristic content of these remaining parts of speech should also be evident.

In this connection the evidence from Anthropological study is very instructive. Among pre-literate[1] people there is the same absence of abstract general terms (Jespersen, 1923, p. 429 *ff*). For instance, the Tasmanians have no word for "tree," but have words for "gum-tree," "wattle-tree," etc.; the Zulus have no word for "cow," but have words for "red-cow," "white-cow," etc. The Cherokees, instead of one word for "washing," have different words according to what is washed. Brinton tells of the poor missionary to an Oregon tribe, who, to convey the idea of "soul," found no word nearer than one which meant "the lower gut."

Of course it is evident that there is a certain amount of abstraction in any symbol, still there is considerable difference between talking about trees in general and this, a particular tree.

On the other hand, words mean action and use, something to be done, as shown so well by Malinowski (1923); the name of a thing means its proper use, and similarly verbs receive their significance in active participation in action. The speech of early humans consisted of "irregular conglomerations;" they expressed whole sentences in a word which might contain a half-dozen different ideas (Jespersen, 1923, p. 421). Brinton (1890, p. 403*f*) from his analysis principally of American languages also concludes

[1] Faris (1925) proposes this term for so-called primitive peoples.

regarding these sentence-words that they partake of the nature of verbs rather than nouns. There is practical agreement upon this word-sentence character of pre-literate speech. Philologists have also pointed out that roots indicate action, they are verbal in nature (Whitney, 1910, p. 260 *ff*; Müller, 1887 ; Romanes, 1889 ; *et al.*). It must be kept in mind, however, that roots are not limited to primitive speech, but belong to all periods. But it is of some significance that all of the words of the voluminous English language can be etymologically reduced to a few roots which are verbal, *i.e.*, express action, rather than nominal in character. The tracing of roots is a very devious process and would not mean much if only one authority came to such conclusions, but there is a wide agreement even among such antagonists as Whitney and Müller, for example.

The facts regarding gesture language among pre-literate peoples also give added data concerning the concrete nature and obvious action content of symbols (see Wundt, 1916, pp. 53–75).

This action content is not without considerable significance for the imitation theory. If words are acquired merely by imitation, why this preponderance of action content, particularly among pre-literate peoples and the lower age groups among children?

The facts and tendencies shown by the material from Barnes are sufficiently clear on their face for the use made of them. However, from a methodological standpoint, it might be worth while to analyse them somewhat more thoroughly.

The marked decrease with age of responses indicating the obvious action content of the symbols has already been commented upon. It was also pointed out that this cannot necessarily be taken as evidence of the decrease of the action content itself. When in the beginning the content of the child's symbols is action, a decrease of obvious action may be accounted for either by the introduction of a greater and greater amount of unexplained " meaning " or by a greater refinement of action content resulting from a more abstract analysis, but still carried on by behaviour processes. As the problem of meaning will be discussed later, and as the present discussion has already furnished evidence of the action content of symbols, the second alternative, viz., that of an increase in more refined behaviour analysis of symbols, which is in line with the behaviouristic hypothesis, may be tentatively accepted.

This decrease of obvious action is most closely associated with age. A Pearsonian correlation gives an r of $-\cdot975$, showing the tendency for the responses to take another form with advancing age. There are only ten items correlated. Yule says there should be at least 15, in order to balance extraneous or chance deviations. Thus in the above correlation there is an opportunity for a large deviation to have undue weight in producing the coefficient. However, allowing for this factor would probably not reduce the r by a significant amount. Furthermore, these percentages are taken from over 37,000 statements and are probably fairly representative. The deviations at 13 and 14 years are probably due to school selection. The deviation at 7 years is apparently due to the fact that the teacher wrote out the responses for the 6-year-old children, thus giving them freer expression, while the task of writing was still difficult for the 7-year-olds who wrote out their own responses. This undoubtedly accounts to some extent for the larger per cent. in unclassified and the smaller proportion of obvious action responses in the 7-year-old group in comparison with the 6 and 8-year groups. If correction could be made for these deviations, it would probably result in a more exact relationship. Taking all these factors into consideration along with the nature of the data and the manner of its selection, it is probable that the above coefficient is somewhere near the true relationship. However, on account of the small number of items and as a check upon the Pearsonian product-moment r, a Spearman rank order coefficient[1] (p) was computed. It gave $p = (-)\cdot986$. Translating this into an r

---

[1] *See* Rugg (1917, pp. 284–92) and Kelley (1923, p. 193).

by Pearson's correction gives $r = (-) \cdot 99$, a slightly higher coefficient than that obtained by the first method.   It is interesting to add the two cases of Binet to the lower end of the series and note the further increase of obvious action with the lower ages (Table VI).   While the validity of comparing two cases with 1,000 can be questioned, the results are as we should expect from a random sample, judging upon the basis of the r already obtained.

TABLE   VI.

ACTION AND USE RESPONSES.

SOURCE TABLES IV AND V.

Age.	Use and Action.	Age.	Use and Action.
3	87	10	62
5	84	11	48
6	82	12	47
7	71	13	37
8	73	14	41
9	68	15	33

The results obtained by Shaw on the study similar to that of Barnes from 600 city children ranging from 8 to 13 years show an increase up to 11 years in both action and use responses.   Shaw thinks this contradicts the results of Barnes.   However, the results are not comparable in this respect.   Shaw's instructions were given in an attempt to get an association response rather than a response showing the content of the stimulus symbol. He thus gets a larger number of categories for classification.   At least two, if not more, of these categories would tend to decrease the action and use percentage in the earlier ages.   Sentence making takes up over 14% at 8 years, but only 2·5% at 13 years, both an absolute and a relative decrease.   This category is bound to be in part a subtraction from use and action.   The case is similar, although not so marked, with the category of possession responses.   It remains fairly constant for 8, 9, 10 years, then has a marked decrease.   Further, Shaw's classification is different from that of Barnes.   His definition of use is much more abstract.   He classifies under action statements which Barnes classifies under use.   In short,

Shaw's data are not contradictory to those of Barnes. If the same use and action category could be segregated, it seems quite probable that it would be similar to that of Barnes up to 11 years as it is after 11 years.

Coefficients, computed from Barnes' data, showing the association of the decrease in obvious action responses with the increase of the tentatively assumed more abstract or refined action responses are given in Table VII. Pearsonian r's were computed. Then, as a check, on account of the small number of items, the Spearman rank order p's were also computed, then translated by Pearson's correction into r coefficients. The results of these two methods corroborate each other.

TABLE VII.

CORRELATION OF OBVIOUS ACTION WITH MORE REFINED ACTION CONTENT.

Responses.	r.	r from p.
Action and Age	—·975	—99
Action and Substance	—·949	—95
Action and Structure	—·946	—95
Action and Form	—·943	—90
Action and Larger Term	—·935	—98
Action and Place	—·804	—76
Action and Quality	—·61	—·61
Action and Colour	+·33	+·44

The inverse association is quite high with all except colour, which is positive, but too low to be of much significance. If the latter were really significant it would be evidence counter to Binet's conclusion regarding visual responses.

The main conclusion remains that in young children the content of symbols is action. With increasing age the obvious action content tends to decrease, while at the same time, apparently, the refined action content increases.

CHAPTER VI

PERSONAL PRONOMINAL SYMBOLS AND SYMBOLIC LEARNING CURVES

WE have been reviewing facts showing the action content in the child's symbols. The examination of the so-called first word as well as other facts indicate this action to be associated with persons. The child's existence is so closely connected with and dependent upon the people among whom—without his leave—he is placed, that symbols to designate others as well as himself are very early and useful acquirements.

Due to the peculiar habit of regarding proper names as "improper" for inclusion in the tabulation of children's vocabularies, the present data are restricted primarily to personal pronouns. They may be taken as one important criterion of the rôle of persons as such in the symbolic behaviour of the child. They also mark a more "personal" aspect of social relationships than has been achieved before their appearance.

In order to follow this inquiry, eight vocabularies were obtained from different sources. Each vocabulary begins with the first word, followed by a record of the new words added each month. They are listed in Table VIII and plotted in Graphs II—IX. On the graphs there are also indicated the personal pronouns and the time of the acquirement of them. An examination of the graphs shows a clear association of the appearance of the personal pronouns with high points in the appearance of new words. Considering only those months in which the data are relatively definite, we find that 78% of the months in which personal pronouns are acquired are associated with a rising curve and that over 85% of such months are associated with peaks or high rates of learning.

TABLE VIII.

THE NUMBER OF NEW WORDS PER MONTH FOR SOME CHILDREN.

Months.	NUMBER OF NEW WORDS.								Months.	CONTINUED.	
	Girl Moyer, 1911.	Girl Nice, 1925.	Girl Bohn, 1914.	Girl Gale, 1900.	Girl Mickens, 1897.	Girl Grant, 1915.	Girl Deville, 1890–91.	Boy Hall, 1896–7.		Moyer, cont.	Nice, cont.
8								I	40	37	117
9	2		I					–	41	23	250
									42	54	↓
10	5		2					2	43	12	
11	x		3					9	44	40	rate
12	1		1			3	4	12			of
13	17		4		3	3	1	14	45	115	106
14	38		21		12	6	4	20	46	43	per
									47	61	mo.
15	x		47	4	12	8	7	48	48	41	
16	x	2	23	5	17	27	21	93	49	30	
17	x	–	49	9	33	30	53	82*			
18	41	–	56	33	39	30	27		50	25	
19	25	–	87	32	26	41	57		51	10	
									52	45	
20	33	1	89	121	45	101	80		53	80	
21	197	–	91	165	24	90	98		54	63	
22	118	1	29	96	70	161	105				
23	90	–	84	147	71	207	98		55	58	
24	1	1	80	129	75	121	113		56	63	
									57	64	
25	65	3	112	x	80	109			58	36	
26	x	4	122	x	80	264			59	7	
27	x	4	68	291	88						
28	x	10		x					60	20	
29	426	2		x					61	19	
									62	x	
30	193	5		477					63	47	
31	122	5							64	57	
32	73	5									
33	72	1							65	42	
34	93	1							66	34	
									67	75	
35	40	3							68	23	
36	103	3							69	45	
37	64	6									
38	72	28							70	26	
39	70	41							71	42	
	cont.	cont.							72	86	

x—no observation.
*—33 for 12 days : at this rate, 82 for 17th month.

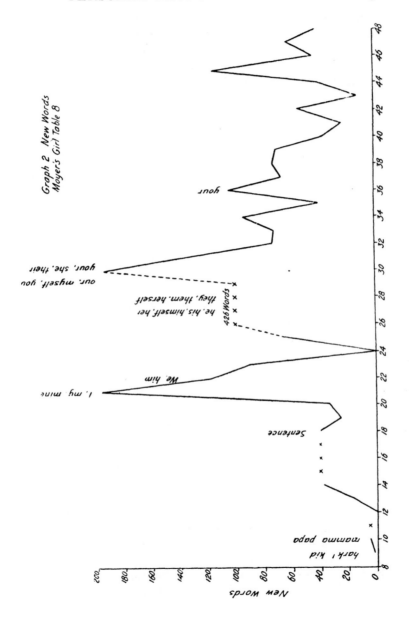

Graph 2 New Words
Moyer's Girl) Table 8

The graphs show that the learning curves are not steady, but have a marked tendency to fluctuate from crests to troughs. It would be very desirable to have other data of the child's activity in order to see how they would correspond with the word-learning curve. It would be

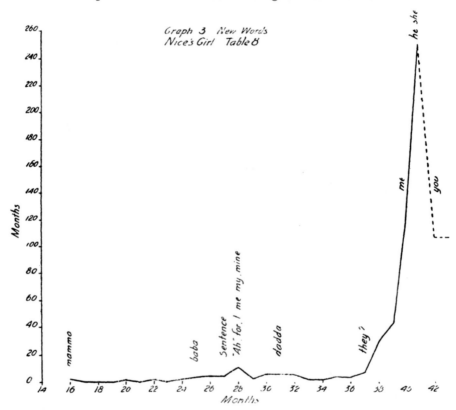

particularly instructive to compare gesture language with vocal language, but sufficient data are not available to do this. Mrs. Nice's child, during the long plateau period, used grunts and gestures. She pointed for food, and when hungry or thirsty, would open her mouth and point to it. It has been a common observation that learning to walk checks or defers language learning. This is probably due to the fact that walking is an act which can be carried out or completed by the child itself, not requiring a great deal of co-operative activity on the part of others.   Such co-operative activity as there is does not necessitate many verbal responses on the part of the child in order to initiate it.   The process of walking may also be quite absorbing to the child.   Some types of motor activity would undoubtedly show a positive correlation with word acquirement.   Watson (1924) has discussed some aspects of the parallel development of motor and speech responses. Judging from the vocabulary curve of Moyer's child, the crest of rapid learning is passed during the third year of life.   The other cases are not for a long enough period to be decisive either way, except to show that there would be a considerable amount of individual variation in this as in other respects.   Figures which Smith (1926, p. 54) gives for 273 children, showing the gain during each six months, show the greatest increase between 2 : 6 and 3 : 0 The figures are :

0 : 6—1 : 0	..	..	..	..	3
1 : 0—1 : 6	..	..	..	..	19
1 : 6—2 : 0	..	..	..	..	250
2 : 0—2 : 6	..	..	..	..	174
2 : 6—3 : 0	..	..	..	..	450
3 : 0—3 : 6	..	..	..	..	326
3 : 6—4 : 0	..	..	..	..	318
4 : 0—4 : 6	..	..	..	..	330
4 : 6—5 : 0	..	..	..	..	202
5 : 0—5 : 6	..	..	..	..	217
5 : 6—6 : 0	..	..	..	..	273

The graphs show a slow or plateau-like start and later a rapid rise in the new word curves.   Usually associated with the beginning of this first rapid rise is the first sentence, as shown by the graphs.   The first sentence, judging by these graphs and other sources,[1] occurs around

[1] *See* Nice (1918), Gheorgov (1905), Stern (1907), and other sources cited here on word learning.

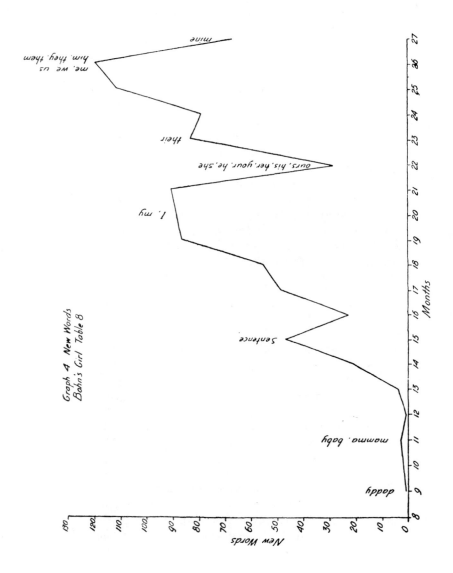

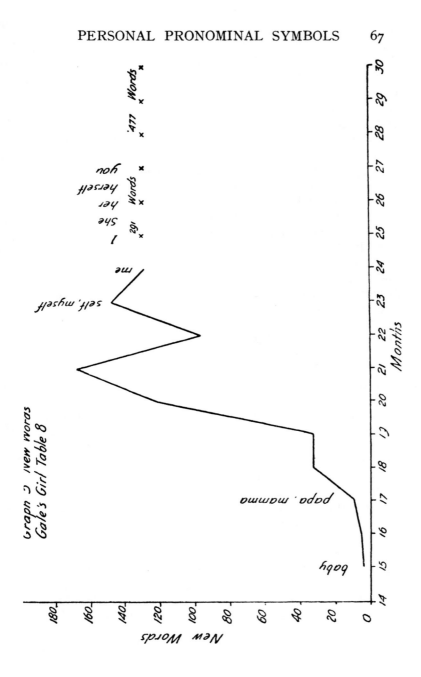

Graph C New Words
Gale's Girl Table 8

the seventeenth month. Koffka and the Sterns say it is about the eighteenth month that the child begins to ask for names, " What 'at ? " and the like. They regard this as a significant point in the child's development.

In so far as we can make an inference from the data available, it would seem to be about or a little before this time when the true language symbol appears. The first genuine sentence, if put together by the child, would mean that symbols were present. It would require an integration in the child's behaviour of separate acts and objects which would necessitate symbols. Of course, it is probably true that some of the so-called first sentences are only parrot verbalizations as are the first words, but these cannot be called true sentences. Also the child's behaviour in asking names shows that symbolic integration is quite well started in its beginning. The beginning rapid rise in the curves are further evidence of a change in the process. However, this appearance of symbols is not to be thought of as an overly sudden development. Word conditioning has been going on for some time.

This conclusion regarding the appearance of the first real symbols at about the seventeenth or eighteenth month was drawn before going into Stern's own study in this connection. It was interesting to find how closely his conclusions concerning the appearance of the first real symbols at 18 months coincided with the above (1907, 1924 Sec. III). In regard to these early symbols, Stern says that the earliest spontaneous remembrances spoken of by Hilde (18 months) referred exclusively to objects, principally persons (1924, p. 378). The differentiation of action, particularly the child's own, a little later (19 months in Hilde's case) is not evidence as might be assumed from Stern's account that these first objects are not action objects. They would be action objects ordinarily in a double sense, due to action on the part of the child and also action on the part of the object, which is generally a person. In the light of all the evidence at hand, it would be hard to show how they could be otherwise

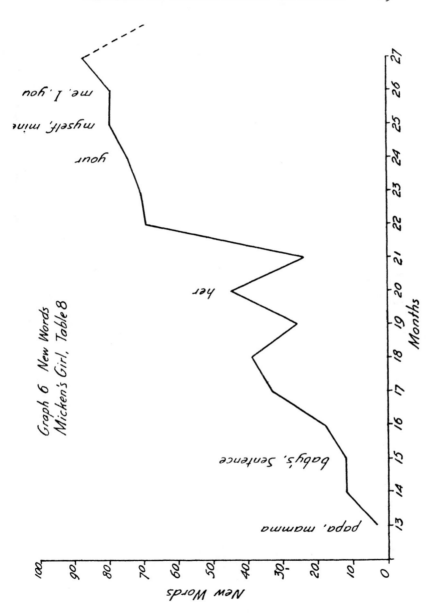

Graph 6 New Words
Micken's Girl, Table 8

F

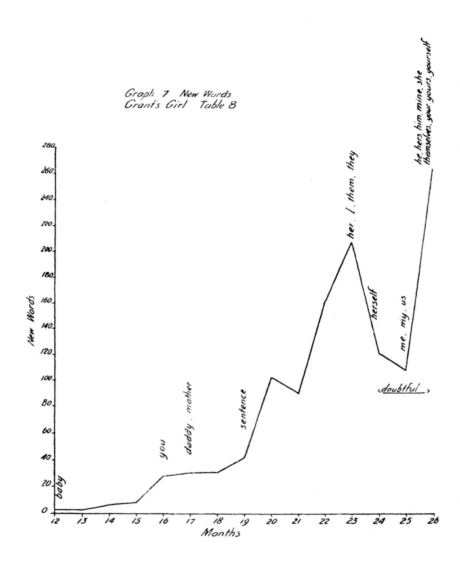

Graph 7   New Words
Grant's Girl   Table 8

than action-objects.[1] To take them as indicating a substance-stage as distinguished from an action-stage seems quite unwarranted. Beginning with such acting objects, the child with more experience becomes able to symbolize actions more distinctly than before, hence greater differentiation develops in this direction. This indicates greater integration, but not a change from a non-action-stage to an action-stage.

As the cases generally studied by child psychologists seem to be somewhat more precocious than the average, the period in which true symbols arise would probably be later for the child population in general. It would be earlier for exceptional children. Such allowances as this must be made for most of the conclusions made regarding periods or stages of development. This, however, does not invalidate such conclusions ; it means that variations may be expected in the application of such generalizations to particular cases. In this connection it is interesting to note that in a study carried on by Muntz in connection with the Yale clinic, Gesell (1925, pp. 217 *seq.*) reports for 50 supposedly normal and representative 2-year-old children of the community in English-speaking homes and of American parentage, that 20, or 40%, used mere words, and 30, or 60%, used sentences. It is probable that these figures cannot be taken without reservations on account of the small amount of check by the observer. It is likely that some of the 40% had used and were capable of using sentences. Nor does the study determine the time of the appearance of the sentence ; thus it might be found that in these cases the average time of its appearance was some months earlier, as is indicated by other observations.

In order to discover which pronouns were acquired first, the list of pronouns were taken in the order in which they were given by the observers. Where several were acquired during one month, some error may be introduced by this procedure. However, from the records it seems that the words were listed in the order in which they occurred during the month. Thus it would be valid to take the

[1] *Cf.* Block, 1923.

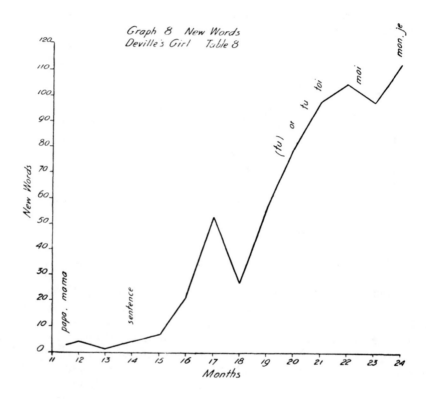

Graph 8 New Words
Deville's Girl Table 8

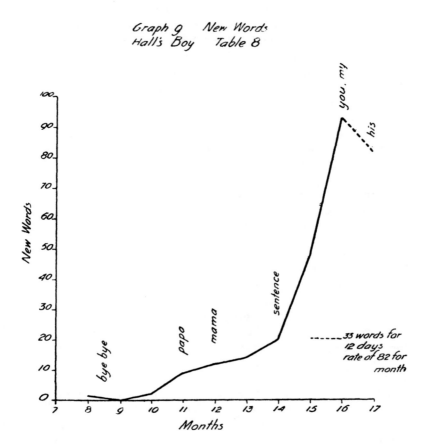

Graph 9   New Words
Hall's Boy   Table 8

listed order as the true order of their appearance during
the month. When only one pronoun is learned during
the month, which happens fairly often, the chance of
misjudging its sequential order would be eliminated. This
would hold true particularly for the first pronouns acquired,
such as " I," " Me," etc. However, four out of the nine
cases considered are daily tabulations, and a fifth case
has the pronouns numbered in the order of their appearance. This would eliminate the risk of such an error for
these cases. The nine cases include seven of those already
given and two from Gheorgov (1905). The data for
Moyer's child were not included on account of the fact
that, although he gives the monthly order of appearance,
the pronouns are not listed according to their appearance
during the month.

It might also be stated that keeping a record of a child's
talk from day to day is a tedious task, with chances
for interruption. These nine cases are probably the
most accurate observations which we have up to the
present.

The results are given in Table IX. They were obtained
by weighting the pronouns in each case according to the
time of appearance. The last one to appear was weighted
1, the next to the last 2, etc. The first one to appear
would thus receive the greatest weight. Having thus
weighted the pronouns, for each child, the total weighting
for any pronoun was obtained by adding together all of
the individual weights for that pronoun. Thus, if, for
three children, " themselves " appeared last, it would be
weighted $1 + 1 + 1 =$ total 3 ; if it appeared last for
one child, next to the last for another, and third from the
last for the other, it would be weighted $1 + 2 + 3 =$
total 6. The number of vocabularies in which a pronoun
occurred is indicated under frequency. The reason for
only nine occurrences of " I " and " Me " is due to the
fact that Mrs. Hall's child was included, for which data
were given to the 500th day only. Just three pronouns
were present, and these were exceptional in that neither
" I " nor " Me " was among them. Mrs. Hall states

that the first pronouns, although used correctly, were not used frequently or independently.

The data of Table IX are summarized in another form in Table X, where they can be more readily analysed.

TABLE IX.
THE ORDER OF THE APPEARANCE OF PERSONAL PRONOUNS.

Pronoun.	Weight.	Frequency.
I	75	8
You	60·5	9
Me	48·5	8
Myself	37	5
Him or her	35	4
My	34	5
Your	26·5	6
He or she	23	4
Yourself	22	4
Himself or herself ...	22	3
Mine	19·5	5
His or hers	18	4
We	17	4
Our	15	2
They	14	2
Them	14	2
Us	12	3
Their	11	2
Themselves	3	1
Ourselves	2	1

TABLE X.
THE ORDER OF THE 1ST, 2ND, AND 3RD PERSONAL PRONOUNS.

1st Person.	2nd Person.	3rd Person.
I	—	—
—	You	—
Me	—	—
Myself	—	—
—	—	Him, or her
My	—	—
—	Your	—
—	—	He or she
—	Yourself	—
—	—	Himself or herself
Mine	—	—
—	—	His or hers
We	—	—
Our	—	—
—	—	They
—	—	Them
Us	—	—
—	—	Their
—	—	Themselves
Ourselves	—	—

It hardly seems justifiable to include in the above computations random observations regarding the appearance of the pronouns. Even serious attempts such as those given above are sufficiently subject to error without introducing other more or less casual observations. However, the following cases from Germany and Poland were taken from Gheorgov's summary to check against the above results. These cases included seven German children observed by : Preyer (one), Linder (two), Ament (one), Frau Friedmann (two), and Frau Baronin (one) ; and one Pole observed by Oltuszewski. They appeared on casual examination perhaps contradictory. It is possible that language differences might change the result. However, a summary of these is corroborative rather than contradictory of the above results. The pronoun " mine " gets a considerably more important place. But in regard to these observations, Gheorgov criticizes some of them very severely, and particularly those connected with the high rating of the possessive " mine." From Table IX it appears that " mine " could easily be moved to a higher place and still leave the results very much the same, comparatively. Thus, while these random observations cannot be included, they appear to be positive rather than negative with reference to the previous data. It would be instructive to make a behaviouristic comparison between different language groups regarding the personal pronouns if materials were available. Pronominal learning might appear somewhat differently in French and English, for example. In the Table already given, only three languages are included : six English children, two Bulgarians, and one French child. These are hardly sufficient for an adequate comparison, but such a comparison would probably leave unchanged the main factors as pointed out (pp. 77 ff). And while it must be kept in mind that the addition of other data might make changes, it is probable that these changes would only be minor ones and would affect only in a minor way the conclusion drawn from these data.

There is a marked tendency for :

   I. The personal pronouns to appear in the order :
1, first person ; 2, second person ; 3, third
person.

  II. The singular pronouns to appear before the plural
pronouns in general and for each series. Gheorgov's material substantiates this for the second
person " you." It is given in both singular and
plural forms in Bulgarian.

 III. The subject-pronoun to appear before the possessive pronoun in each case.

 IV. The pronoun ending in " self " or " selves " to
appear late in each series ; *i.e.,* in the first person
singular, first person plural, etc.

  V. The subject " I," " we," and " they " to appear
before the object " me," " us," and " them."

 A. This is probably true for the second personal
pronoun " you," but cannot be decided for these
data because of the double use of " you " as
subject and object. The subject " you " appears
before the object " you " for Gheorgov's data,
although the time between is relatively short.

 B. The instance of the object " him " or " her " before
the subject " he " or " she " is probably due to
the fact that the child is used to having himself
referred to frequently in the objective case as
" him " or " her."

The outstanding feature of these observations is the
appearance of the pronouns which designate persons as
subjects before those which designate persons as objects
or with possessive reference. Now the important question
is, What is the significance of these speech reactions in
this respect ?

The first and correct answer is that there must be more
careful research before we shall be able to determine with
desirable certainty.

It has been observed that children, when first learning
personal pronouns, may get them mixed. A child may
say, for instance, " You gave it to her," or " You went

walking," and the like meaning itself in both cases ; or it will say " I " meaning " you." However, this sort of mistake is not surprising. On the other hand, children do use these pronouns correctly and these mistakes must not be overemphasized.

The facts above, showing that the later pronouns also follow this same order—subject, object, and possessive forms—lend support to the supposition that the child designates himself " I " as a subject before he designates himself as an object or as a possessor in so far as the pronominal designations are concerned. This order of the acquirement of the personal pronouns quite probably indicates the actual order, although not the beginning, of the integration of the self in its relation to others.

It would, of course, be quite naïve and illegitimate to claim, as some have done, that the first integration of the child as a self arises only with the first personal pronoun. As soon as the first real symbol appears there must be some sort of personal differentiation involved in the behaviour of the child, particularly if the social factor is as important as has already been indicated. Even before the first symbol the child in his habits of adjustment has established a basis in action for such a differentiation of himself. He already has a " parrot " name for himself and begins some symbolic self-reference when the self and symbols have arisen, before the pronoun " I " appears.

It must be insisted upon that the mere appearance of one pronoun or another is not the real point ; it is only, as these pronouns indicate other facts and conditions of social experience, that they are significant. Thus, concerning the first personal pronoun, it is the designation by the child of itself as in an active state which is important. And this use of the " I " to indicate the acting child is the significant aspect pointing to a behaviouristic content of this primary self symbol. In such an active organism other aspects of the self and personality are later integrated and symbolized. It is probable that whatever self name or whatever self pronoun appears first is used predominantly in this self-acting reference and that the " me," or more passive self, develops later as a *differentiation of* this primary self as indicated by our data.

Some other facts also point to the significance of the early appearance of " I " in these cases. It has been noted by observers that first-born children do not use " I " until late. Older children seem to stimulate the younger child to acquire this pronoun early and to use it quite correctly (Stern, 1924, p. 157). At least four of these children, a child of Gheorgov, of Deville, of Bohn, and of Grant, appear to be the first or only child. Mrs. Hall's evidently was an only child, but it lived for a time at least with other children. The data are incomplete concerning Micken's child, but it is probable that it had association with children. The three other cases are those of later children. Thus with these only children included in the computation the " I " pronoun ranks first. Gheorgov thinks it quite significant that " I " appeared first for both of his sons in spite of the fact that Bulgarians have a tendency to leave off the " I " pronoun in speaking.

The appearance of the subject reference before the possessive reference also probably indicates a significant situation. There are conflicting observations regarding the early possessive habits of the child. Watson's work on children goes to indicate that there is not much in the way of a possessive instinct. Any sort of inherent propensities which a child might have would seem to be comparable to those of other animals which constitute a rather slim outfit. From this genetic viewpoint, there is little evidence for presuming much of a native basis for possessive habits. The more fundamental are the manipulative acts and those pertaining to the consumption of things. A young child is much more apt to destroy, throw away, or to stick into his mouth and try to eat than to keep as a possession. Judged from these facts, it would seem natural that the subject " I " should develop before the possessive " my " or " mine " as our data indicate. This would seem to show that our general possessive activity is based upon an earlier development of the social

" self " and that they are consequently built up and established by social training and inculcation. This, however, is a problem for further research.

From the summary it will be noticed that " you " also appears very early. If the explanation of the integration of symbols given in Chapter III is correct, this early appearance of " you " would also be expected in addition to the other more specific designations for persons. The " I " and " you " are evidently very closely connected.

The average time at which the " I " appeared was about the end of the 23rd month. The " you," on the average, appeared about the end of the 24th month. In this connection it is instructive to compare the appearance of the pronouns with some of Stern's conclusions. His first period of language development is from 12 to 18 months ; the second is from 18 to 24 months, in which true symbols develop rapidly ; the third period is from 24 to 30 months, during which the child learns inflections and finer shades of expression. At two years, he says, words being " to live, to bend, to move " (1924, p. 165). As indicated, it is also at the second year mark or a trifle before, according to the data analysed here, that the personal pronouns appear. It is probable that the explanation for the beginning of this new period is to be found in the greater differentiation produced by social activity. A more " personal " integration in the child's behaviour, effected by social contact and interaction, has served to set his " self " off more clearly from " others," to mark his acts off from the acts of others. What he is doing becomes more definitely separated from what others are doing. For illustration, instead of " Mamma—eat," it becomes more clearly distinct as " Mamma gives bread—Baby eat," " Mamma eat—Susan eat," and the like. Social contacts and experience also serve to differentiate acts which are past from present acting, and also from future ones. Not that there is a clear time sense, but there is some sequential differentiation in one direction or another. Such a social integration would lay a basis in experience for the acquirement of the personal pronouns, inflections, and the like.

Another way of getting at the significance of the pronouns is the actual use which is made of them by the child in his social life.   This will be a main consideration of the next chapter.

CHAPTER VII

The Use of Personal Symbols

To continue the study of the rôle of persons in the symbolic development of the child, materials on the ordinary speech activity of children were obtained. While the acquirement of a symbol may be significant, the further use of it in the behaviour processes of the child is also an important aspect of the integration of symbols.

The great amount of energy expended in speech reactions is illustrated by Table XI on all-day conversations.

The averages for ten cases are as follows :—

Years of age	3·4
Total words spoken	11,518
Words per minute	15·6

Averages for six of these cases are :—

Different words used	795·7
Use of each word	13·8

Averages for five of these cases are :—

Total per cent. of vocabulary used	41·3
Number of sentences	2,049
Words per sentence	5·6

Brandenburg states that his 4⅓-year-old child was linguistically inactive only 19 minutes during the whole day of 12 hours (outside of 20 minutes in the library). These conversations appear to be taken in a home environment very favourable to speech activity. For instance, in a study of 18 children in the Merrill-Palmer school,

TABLE XI.

COMPARISON OF ALL-DAY CONVERSATIONS.

Authority.		Child.	Age. Years.	Total Words.	Words per Minute.	Different Words.	% of Vocabulary.	Average Use of each word.	No. of Sentences.	Average Words in Sentence.
Gale	...	Boy C	2	10,507	15·2	805	—	13·0	—	—
Gale	...	Boy S	2½	9,290	13·4	751	52·5	12·4	—	—
Gale	...	Girl H	2½	8,992	13	629	41·6	14·3	—	—
Nice	...	Girl D	3	7,600	10·6	—	—	—	2,018	3·77
Brandenburg	...	Girl G	3	11,628	16	859	34	13·7	1,873	6·6
Bell	...	Girl A	3½	15,230	21	—	—	—	—	—
Nice	...	Girl R	4	11,511	13·4	731	54·5	14·4	2,686	3·9
Brandenburg	...	Girl G	4	14,930	20	999	24	14·9	1,967	7·5
Bell	...	Girl B	4½	14,992	20	—	—	—	—	6·17
Nice	...	Girl E	5	10,500	13·4	—	—	—	1,702	—
Average	...		3·4	11,518	15·6	795·7	41·3	13·8	2,049	5·59

Source Nice, 1920, p. 168.

made by Marion Mattson (1926), the average of words per minute is lower. There were two groups of nine children in each ; the ages of Group I were from 35–40 months, average 37·4, and the ages of Group II were from 51–56, average 55·4. Excluding one case, age 37 months, in Group I, which hardly talked at all while at school, saying only 46 words in 540 hours' observation, the average for the 17 children is 6·7 words per minute. Just how much difference there is between verbal activity at school and at home it is difficult to say, but evidently there is considerable difference. If the average for the whole day were available, it would undoubtedly be much greater and would probably be still greater for children not in a nursery school. According to Miss Mattson, nursery school children are apt to talk less. The period of observation was limited in any one day to three hours.

The percentages of the different parts of speech of the conversations of some children are given in Table XII ; the prepositions, conjunctions and interjections are small in number and are not included. The figures are taken from Boyd (1914), Nice (1920), and two samples I took and classified from the all-day conversation of Brandenburg's 40-month-old child (1915). Boyd's data were obtained by recording the sentences during the last week of the month ; the others represent all-day conversations, except that hour conversations only are reported for two of Nice's children.

Any such classification of a child's speech into the conventional forms of grammar is bound to be forced. An attempt to do it will convince the most sceptical of the truth of this statement. This fact must be kept in mind when considering the following figures. They can only be taken as indicating certain general conditions rather than precise measurements. The summary of the usage of different parts of speech (Tables XII and XIII) shows that verbs hold first place, pronouns second, and nouns third. The adverbs and adjectives are about even, with the adverbs maintaining a slightly higher rank, as will appear from an examination of the original percent-

TABLE XII.

THE PARTS OF SPEECH OF CHILDREN'S CONVERSATION IN PERCENTAGES OF TOTAL WORDS USED.

Parts of Speech.	CHILD AND AGE IN YEARS.							
	Boyd	Boyd	Nice	Brandenburg Sample	Boyd	Nice Child R	Nice Child R[1]	Nice
	2	3	3	3⅓	4	4	4	5
	% of Total	% of Total	% of Total	% of Total	% of Total	% of Total	% of Total	% of Total
(1)	(2)	(3)	(4)	(5)	(6)	(7)	(8)	(9)
Verbs ...	27·7	22·6	23·1	26—29	21·1	28·2	29·6	28·1
Pronouns	6·2	15·8	22·3	21—22	18·1	22·1	23·1	22·8
Nouns	36·8	16·4	17·3	17	14·8	19·5	19·4	15·8
Adverbs	13·2	9·4	18·6	16	11·6	16·0	14·0	10·2
Adjectives	13·7	17·4	9·3	9	14·6	8·6	7·6	13·7

Source : Boyd, 1914 ; Nice, 1920 ; Brandenburg, 1915.

TABLE XIII.

THE RANK OF PARTS OF SPEECH ACCORDING TO USAGE.

Parts of Speech.	THE RANKING IN COLUMNS TABLE XII.							
	(2)	(3)	(4)	(5)	(6)	(7)	(8)[1]	(9)
Verbs ...	2	1	1	1	1	1	1	1
Pronouns	5	4	2	2	2	2	2	2
Nouns ...	1	3	4	3	3	3	3	3
Adverbs ...	4	5	3	4	5	4	4	5
Adjectives	3	2	5	5	4	5	5	4

Source : Table XII.

ages. These data are also corroborated by Smith's study (1926) on 101 children from 2 to 5 years. Her figures are :

Number of Children and Age Group.

	19—2 yrs.	28—3 yrs.	32—4 yrs.	22—5 yrs.
	%	%	%	%
Verbs ..	26 ± 7	27 ± 6	26 ± 5	27 ± 6
Pronouns ..	16 ± 6	25 ± 6	24 ± 5	25 ± 6
Nouns ..	22 ± 6	16 ± 5	15 ± 4	15 ± 5
Adverbs ..	21 ± 6	15 ± 5	13 ± 4	11 ± 4
Adjectives ..	5 ± 3	7 ± 3	11 ± 4	12 ± 5

[1] Same child as column (7), but based upon one hour out of the day.

G

Ranking these figures for the different ages, we obtain the following :—

	2 years.	3 years.	4 years.	5 years.
Verbs ..	1	1	1	1
Pronouns ..	4	2	2	2
Nouns ..	2	3	3	3
Adverbs ..	3	4	4	5
Adjectives ..	5	5	5	4

A remarkable fact brought out here is that the pronouns, although composing only a very small percentage of the vocabulary, usually around 2 or 3 per cent., hold second place in actual usage after the two-year ages.

The nouns, which usually predominate in the known vocabulary, hold third place in actual usage. The importance of action in a child's speech behaviour is again shown by the predominance in the use of verbs. The high percentage of verbs may be partially due to the structure of language. This, however, would not detract from the action character of symbolic behaviour. Language structure itself must be looked upon as being determined by symbolic behaviour, and hence its structure would reflect the action character of such behaviour. Thus, from this standpoint, these percentages would be significant as indicating the action content. It would be valuable to obtain a comparison of children's conversations with those of adults in order to discover the relative differences. Tracy (1909, Ch. V) concludes that there is a decrease in the use of verbs in adult verbal activity and random observation would seem to substantiate this. However, more exact and reliable comparison is necessary before definite conclusions can be drawn in this respect. The higher percentage of adverbial usage at earlier ages also emphasizes the action character. If the previous inductions regarding the action content of nouns are generalized to include these data under consideration, further weight is given to the significance of action content in the child's speech behaviour.

Observations show this action content to be associated

to a very large degree with persons, indicated by the
personal pronominal symbols and by other personal
symbols   The verbs and pronouns alone make up approximately 50% or more of the total words used by the
children under consideration, with the exception of the
two-year ages.   The lower figure for two years is accounted
for by the fact that these children are just beginning to
acquire pronouns.   Boyd's child is apparently somewhat
atypical in this respect.   While all pronouns are not
personal pronouns, they are predominantly so in a child's
vocabulary.   Some idea of the proportion of personal
pronouns to the pronouns may be obtained from Table
XIV.   Even at two years for Boyd's child, 61% of the
pronouns were personal pronouns ;   at three and four

TABLE XIV.
RELATION OF PERSONAL PRONOUNS TO PRONOUNS.

| Child. | Age Years. | PER CENT. OF TOTAL WORDS. | | % of Personal Pronouns[3] of Pronouns. |
		Pro- nouns.	Personal Pronouns.	
Boyd	2	6·2	3·78	60·96
Boyd	3	15·8	13·34	84·4
Boyd ...	4	18·1	14·91	82·4
Brandenburg[1]	3	21–22	15·12	69–72
Nice D ...	3	22·3	" I " alone 7·67	34·4
Nice D ...	3		I omitted 18 times if includ- ed ... 9·67	43·4
Nice R ...	4	22·1	1st p.p. 11·76	53·2
			2nd p.p. 2·00	9·0
			1 and 2 13·76	62·3
Nice R ...	4[2]	23·1	" I " alone 9·98	43·2
Nice E ...	5	22·8	" I " alone 6·19	27·1
Mattson : (1926)	Group I— 9 children, 36–20 months.		15·6	
	Group II— 9 children, 51–56 months.		18·1	

[1] Summarized from his data (1915).
[2] Based upon only one hour's conversation.
[3] In cases indicated these figures do not include all personal pronouns.

years, the figures were 84 and 82 respectively. Brandenburg's $3\frac{1}{3}$-year-old child had about 70% of the pronouns personal pronouns.

Brandenburg (1915) published the all-day conversation of his child at $3\frac{1}{3}$ years. In his summary he gives only a partial list of the pronouns. In order to get the complete list I tabulated them. My figures are considerably different from his. This leads me to question his figures for both $3\frac{1}{3}$ and $4\frac{1}{3}$ years regarding pronouns. However, assuming that he made the same error on both sets of data, they are probably comparable for the comparison which is made in another connection (Table XVII, Graph 10). The figures which I obtained are used in Tables XIV and XV. Allowing for chance errors, these figures should be quite accurate.

Three cases in Table XIV show " I " alone forming from 27 % to 43% of the total pronouns. In one case, only the first and second personal pronouns compose 62%.

The percentage which the personal pronouns make of the total number of words used for the ages three years and above, Table XIV, is 13 % to 18%. As Boyd's child is atypical, the 13% is undoubtedly lower than usual. Nice says that her child R used " I " for the subject in 36% of the sentences. Brandenburg says that his child at $4\frac{1}{3}$ used the first personal pronoun in some form in 50% of the sentences.

Further, in regard to the relation of verbs to the personal pronouns, Drevers found that of the verbs in the known vocabulary of his three children a great majority referred to the action of self or to self—the figures show 72% to 89% (Table XVI).

In checking over the all-day conversation published by Brandenburg, the information was not sufficient for one to be able to make anything but an approximate estimate ; it was found that at least 80% or more of the sentences were concerned with the self and persons, the great majority of them indicating action.

The data obtained indicate a very definite association of symbolic behaviour with personal references.

So far we have not considered in particular another set of facts, the persons designated by nouns. The use of names of persons, such as " papa," " mamma," etc., also comprise a significant part of speech activity. In analysing Brandenburg's data, I found words for persons besides the pronouns amounted to 503. This raises the percentage of words for persons to over 19. Mattson's data show approximately 23% of the total words are personal symbols, counting double designations such as Charlie

TABLE XV.

BRANDENBURG'S CHILD-PRONOUNS.

Personal Pronouns.					Number.
1st P.P. Sing.	...	...	...	...	...	1116
2nd P.P. Sing.	...	...	...	...	...	433
1st P.P. Plural	...	...	...	...	...	106
3rd P.P. Sing.[1]	...	...	...	...	...	103
3rd P.P. Plural[1]	...	...	...	...	...	54

Source : Data summarized by Markey (Brandenburg, 1915).

TABLE XVI.

ACTION IN RELATION TO SELF.

Source : Drevers (1915).

Child.				Age.		% of Action to or of Self.
Boy H	...	...	...	28 months	...	88·7
Girl D	...	...	...	43 months	...	82·7
Boy J	...	...	...	54·5 months	...	72·4

Chaplin as only one personal symbol. Mrs. Horn's data for kindergarten children all over the country, the conversations totalling 489,555 words used, show 16·6% are personal designations, not including practically all proper names, and all words which were spoken less than 41 times. The proper names, with the exception of a few characters of more than local note, were excluded altogether, and the published list did not give words below 41 frequencies. If proper names plus the personal symbols below this frequency were included, it would undoubtedly raise the

[1] These contain personal pronouns designating a dog, chicken, etc. : he—12, she—2, him—4, they—21, them—20 = 59. Forty-one of the third plural are not personal in the sense that they designated persons. A negligible number of the " you " pronouns were used to indicate other than a person.   However, sociologically we know that animals and even toys are personal objects for the child.

percentage to over 20. Judging from these figures, the percentage for the use of personal symbols (including pronouns) for these early ages is apparently slightly more than 20% of the total words used.

Returning to the use of the personal pronouns, their relation among themselves is noteworthy. Beginning at about 24 months, the use of them increases rapidly until they make up a good percentage of the spoken words, according to Mattson's data about 15% at 3 + years and about 18% at 4 + years. All but two of her cases had an I. Q. of 100 or better, most of them above this; so that the groups are weighted somewhat in the upper half of the I. Q. scale.

In computing and comparing percentages, using the total words as a base, showing the use of the 1st, 2nd, and 3rd personal pronominal symbols for Boyd's child, some significant facts came to light (Table XVII and Graph 10, Fig. A). The first personal singular pronouns held first place and increased rapidly in use until the third year, when they began to decrease relatively. The second personal pronouns started much lower, increased slowly, and were still rising at four years. The first person plural pronouns started still lower and were also increasing at four years. The third personal pronouns were somewhat below the second personal pronouns in use. The figures of Nice, Brandenburg, and also those of Drevers (Table XVI) on the verbs in relation to self also show similar tendencies, a decrease in the first person singular pronouns and a further increase in the other pronouns after three years (Table XVII, Graph 10). Nice's child R began talking very late, which undoubtedly accounts for the high figure for it at four years. On this account it might be taken as substantiating the hypothesis, for having started late (*see* Graph 3) it would be reaching the peak of " self " reference approximately a year later than usual. There is a substantial decrease between D, three years, and E, five years, the other two children.

It is questionable, however, whether three children, even in the same family, can be compared in this manner with assurance that the resulting curves are typical. Consequently, both Nice's and Drevers' figures comparing these children at different ages must not be taken as having much significance unless it is assumed that each child is normal and typical in the points compared. This is probably so regarding Drevers' children ; he uses them for purposes of making comparisons. From Mrs. Nice's account, her children D and E are apparently sufficiently normal in speech development for this comparison between them. Mattson's data, which I have summarized in Table XVIII and Graph 11 further corroborate these findings for a larger number of children. The "self" pronouns decrease after three years and the "other" pronouns increase.

TABLE XVII.

THE RELATIVE RISE AND FALL IN THE USE OF THE "SELF" AND THE CONTINUED RISE IN THE "OTHER" PRONOUNS.

Child.			Age. Years.	PERSONAL PRONOUNS—% OF TOTAL WORDS USED.			
				1st Sing.	2nd.	1st Plur.	3rd.
Boyd	...	...	2	2·4	·10	·012	·00
Boyd	...	...	3	6·86	1·91	·26	1·96
Boyd	...	...	4	6·05	2·80	·78	2·21
Brandenburg		...	3½	7·34		3·23	
Brandenburg		...	4½	6·32	3·32	·54	—
				" I "	" You "		
Nice D	...	...	3	7·67	1·67	—	—
Nice R	...	...	4	9·97	1·77	—	—
Nice E	...	...	5	6·19	2·21	—	—

Source : Nice, 1920 ; Boyd, 1914 ; Brandenburg, 1915.

There is considerable fluctuation in both Group I and Group II (see Table XVIII and Graph 11), so that the trend, although definite for these cases, might not be reliable if generalized to other cases. Two facts in regard to these data must be considered with reference to the validity of using them as a basis for judgment regarding other groups. (1) The number of cases is small, being

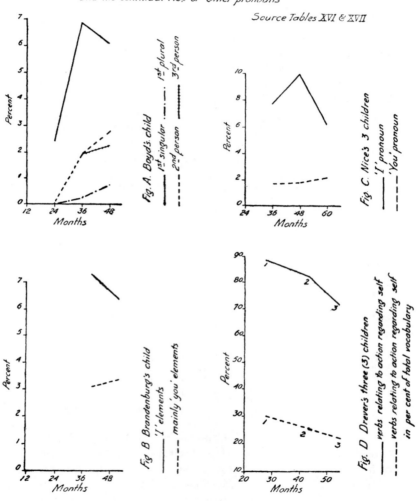

Graph 10   Showing the peak of 'Self' pronouns at three years
           and the continual rise of 'Other' pronouns

Source Tables XVI & XVII

Fig. A. Boyd's child
1st singular —— 1st plural ——·——
2nd person ———— 3rd person ········

Fig. C. Nice's 3 children
'I' pronoun ——
'You' pronoun ————

Fig. B Brandenburg's child
'I' elements ——
mainly 'you' elements ————

Fig. D Drever's three (3) children
verbs relating to action regarding self ——
verbs relating to action regarding self ————
in per cent of total vocabulary

limited to 18. Allowance must be made for this fact and the figures should be checked by various methods when possible. Consequently, in addition to the product-moment coefficients of correlation, the rank order coeffi-

TABLE XVIII.

SHOWING THE DECREASE IN " SELF " AND THE CONTINUED INCREASE IN " OTHER " PRONOUNS AFTER THREE YEARS.

Child.	M.A.[3] Months.	Aver. Words per Minute.	Total Different Words 540 hrs.	PERSONAL PRONOUNS.				
				1st Sing.	2nd Per.	1st Plur.	3rd Sing.	3rd Plur.
Group I :								
A	41	·09	25	15·2	—	—	—	—
E	33	·59	99	7·5	1·3	—	—	—
D	39	2·01	166	15·1	2·3	·1	·9	1·2
C	41	2·08	(162)[1]	13·6	1·6	·8	1·5	·4
B	37	3·41	231	15·4	1·1	·2	·3	·1
F	37	4·39	268	10·2	2·7	·5	·6	·0
H	50	4·78	330	12·1	2·2	·6	·0	·7
G	43	5·23	447	12·3	3·9	·7	·6	·5
I	56	6·30	440	9·6	2·9	·8	·4	·9
Average	41·9	3·21	—	12·3	2·0	·4	·5	·4
Group II :								
D	66	4·52	324	15·3	3·7	·0	·0	·0
E	70	5·89	479	10·4	3·9	·9	·9	·3
F	71	7·80	609	10·0	4·1	1·4	1·2	·6
A	60	9·07	(290)[2]	14·1	2·8	·7	1·0	·1
G	53	10·15	593	11·6	4·6	1·4	·6	·6
H	62	10·19	689	9·3	4·1	1·2	2·9	·4
B	68	11·85	(442)[2]	9·1	5·9	·8	1·0	·6
I	74	12·00	739	9·6	4·5	2·0	1·2	·7
C	69	13·34	735	11·1	4·0	1·9	1·4	·6
Average	65·9	9·42	—	11·2	4·2	1·1	1·1	·4

Source : computed from Mattson's data (1926).

cients *p* have also been computed. (2) The groups do not represent a random sample of the population. However, barring a few cases which had to be left out on account of absence or illness, these two groups include all the children in the school falling within the age limits selected. Thus,

[1] 360 hours.　　[2] 180 hours.　　[3] M.A.=Mental age.

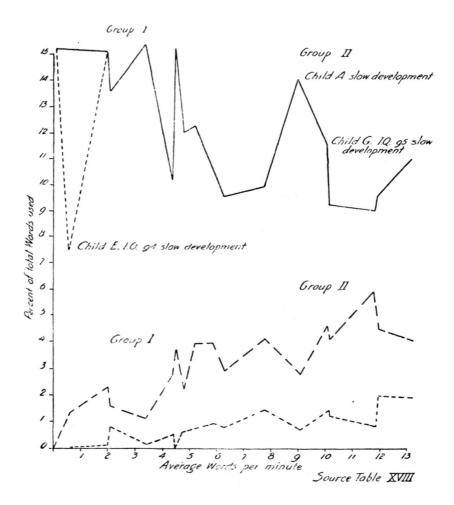

Graph II Showing the decrease in the use of the 'Self' pronoun and the
increase in the use of the 'Other' pronouns after three years
Legend_____ 'Self' pronouns
— — — 'You' pronouns
- - - - - - 'We' pronouns

Group 1

Group II

Child A slow development

Child G. IQ. 95 slow
development

Child E. I.Q. 94 slow development

Group II

Group 1

Percent of total Words used

1 2 3 4 5 6 7 8 9 10 11 12 13
Average Words per minute

Source Table XVIII

although these cases cannot be considered as random samples of the population, most of them also being average or above in mental age, still, if they can be considered as random samples or representative of similar groups at these ages, it would be legitimate to apply the laws of probability to them as representative of such other groups. It will at least be instructive to do so.

In order to test whether there is a significant difference between the mean of Group I and Group II, and thus a real trend, the Standard Error (ϵ) was computed for the difference, for this first singular series. One case, E in Group I, was decidedly abnormal in its speech development in this respect. Consequently, it was excluded in this computation. The report from its parents said that its speech development was slow, that it did not begin to use " meaningful " words until about 24 months. It was an only child, and generally played alone while at home. This would tend to retard speech development. Its mental age was 33, with an I. Q. of 94. In order to test the hypothesis regarding the decrease in the use of " self " pronouns after three years, it would be necessary to exclude cases of such slow speech development as well as the ages much below 36 months, on account of the fact that they might still be on the upward trend of the cycle. This case was excluded in all the computations involving the "self" symbol, but not otherwise. With the other pronouns, it would take its regular rank without danger of throwing off the computation.

The ϵ with this case excluded is 1·15 and $M_1 - M_2 =$ 1·7. The difference between the means is larger than the ϵ, but if the difference is not greater than $3 \times \epsilon$, then this difference may be due to sampling. Consequently, we cannot be statistically sure whether this difference between the means and the consequent trend is due to chance or actually represents a general situation among similar groups. On other statistical and extra-statistical grounds, however, our conclusion is that the difference is significant. The other data, particularly those on individual cases, show the same trend. Individual variation in reaching the peak, or the crest, of the cycle in the use of self pronouns would of itself cause a substantial amount of the Standard Error. One child would reach the high point earlier and another later than usual, thus causing variation in the downward trend regardless of a similar cycle in each case. Furthermore, the large ϵ may be due primarily to the number of cases which, if increased, might reduce it markedly. But it seems evident that there is a great amount of individual variation between children in the time at which they reach the high point in the use of " self " pronouns. This seems to be the real explanation of a large part of the variation. For the second person, or " you " series, the figures are $M_1 - M_2 = 2 \cdot 2 \pm \epsilon \cdot 447$. This is greater than $3 \times \epsilon$, and is thus statistically significant. For the first plural, or " we " series, the figures are $M_1 - M_2 = \cdot 7 \pm \epsilon \cdot 223$, which is also greater than $3 \times \epsilon$.

Computations were not performed for the third person series. The third singular appears somewhat similar, but less consistent than the " we " series, and the third plural is apt to be unreliable, due to their usage for so-called impersonal objects. The percentages are also quite low.

In order to obtain another measure of the trend, a Pearsonian Frequency correlation between the decrease in " self " pronominal reference and mental age was computed. The results are $r = -\cdot 34 \pm$ P.E. $\cdot 145$. The r is a little above $2 \times$ P.E. and, although not as statistically reliable as it should be, is nevertheless some indication that the r may be due to a true association to be found among similar groups. The r itself is low, however, indicating again a great deal of fluctuation in relation to mental age. But what evidence there is does confirm the hypothesis.

In order to test it further, a Pearsonian Frequency correlation between the decrease in the " self " pronominal reference and the average number of words spoken per minute was computed. The results were $r = -\cdot 636 \pm$ P.E. $\cdot 097$. This latter r is high enough to be quite significant as well as being far beyond the P.E. Thus, in

this case, association is seen to be quite close and statistically reliable as a basis for judging this association in other
similar groups.

From these correlations we conclude that there is the
decrease in the use of the " self " pronouns after three
years, but that, instead of being so closely associated with
mental age, it is more directly associated with the average
number of words used per minute, for these cases.

The question is, what is the significance of these figures ?
If the use of words can be taken as a rough measure of
symbolic integration, then the " self " reference decreases
as symbolic integration increases.   Reasons for assuming
that the average number of words is such an index should
be fairly evident.

The fact that the child learns words and their significance
by using them and by stimulating both himself and others
to respond to them shows the use of words to be very
important.   It seems that this might be more true of the
child than the adult, because the child is just learning
symbols, and their overt use must be a large factor in this
process.   Further weight is added to this assumption due
to the fact that there is a very close association observable
between the average words used per minute and the
number of different words used.   The correlation coefficient is $r = + \cdot 954 \pm$ P.E. 0·24.   Only 15 cases were
used to obtain the r, as three cases out of the 18 were not
observed for the same length of time as were the rest.
They were consequently not comparable, nor could they
be made so by a proportion ratio.   It is known that
the total vocabulary, as determined by vocabulary tests,
correlated very highly with mental age.   The total
vocabulary score of a child is, according to Terman, a
very good index, especially at lower ages, of intelligence
level.   He finds a correlation of ·91 between M.A. and total
vocabulary score for children from Grade I to the first
grade high school.   For adults the same coefficient is
somewhat lower, ·81.   He states, " We believe it will be
possible, before long, to measure the intelligence level

almost as accurately by means of 100 crucial words as it can now be measured by any existing intelligence scale " (1918, p. 464). The correlation between the average words per minute and mental age for these data is + ·725, also indicating a close relationship. All of these facts tend to show the significance of this measure as a criterion of symbolic development.

It might be said that it is to be expected that with the larger number of words used, the less proportionally will be the use of " self " pronouns. But this is not true before three years, while the use of these pronouns is reaching its peak. Nor is it true for " other " personal pronouns even after three. Further, it is exactly this point which is being emphasized ; namely, that the relative place of " self " reference does diminish with the greater use of words with greater symbolic integration, and that symbolic behaviour becomes concerned with other persons and objects to a greater and greater degree.

Further information showing the use of words to be an important criterion of symbolic integration appears in other chapters, particularly in Chapter IX on the nature of symbolic integration.

It is possible that by taking these observations in the nursery school environment, justice may not have been done to each child, and consequently more favourable conditions would give data showing even higher correlations. However, due to the fact that all figures were obtained in a similar manner, they probably do depict the situation fairly well, if not in the most accurate manner. But if a more accurate measure of symbolic integration were available, it is probable that the correlation of " self " reference with this measure would be considerably beyond − ·616.

Partial correlation throws some light upon this association. To obtain a correlation between the decrease in the use of " self " pronouns and symbolic integration, as represented by the average use of words per minute uninfluenced by mental age, a partial correlation was computed by holding M.A constant. The result was an

r 12·3 $= -$ ·60, which is very close to the r already obtained, and gives still further evidence of the negative association after three years of the use of " self " pronouns with symbolic integration. In the partial correlation the coefficients given in Table XIX were used.

TABLE XIX.

THE CORRELATION OF PRONOMINAL USAGE WITH MENTAL AGE AND THE
AVERAGE WORDS USED PER MINUTE.

	Series Correlated.	r	P.E.	p	r^1 from p
1	Use of Self Pronouns with M.A., 17 items[2]	—·34	±·145	—·55208	—·57
2	Use of Self Pronouns with A.W. per minute, 17 items ...	—·636	±·097	—·6979	—·71
3	M.A. with A.W. per minute, 18 items ...	+·725	±·076	+·7966	+·81
4	Use of Self Pronouns with A.W. per minute M.A. held constant using r's of 1, 2, 3 above ...	—·60		—·515	
5	Use of " You "[3] pronouns with A.W. per minute, 18 items ...	+·855	±·043	+·8751	+·88
6	Use of " We "[3] pronouns with A.W. per minute, 18 items ...	+·85	±·044	+·856	+·87
7	ηxy for same as 2 above ; x and y are same as for Graph II	(—)·858			
8	ηxy corrected for too fine groupings[4] ...	(—)·76	±·069		
9	Test for linearity $\eta^2 xy - r^2$	(—)·173	±·430		
10	ηyx for sale as 2 above (see 7)	·639	±·097		
11	A.W. per minute with number of different words, 15 items ...	+·954	±·024	+·982	+·98

Source of data, Table XVIII.

When looking over the frequency distribution, the correlation appears to be slightly non-linear (*see* Graph 11). This characteristic is further emphasized when cases A

[1] From Pearson's formula.   [3] All forms.
[2] Case E excluded.   [4] *See* Kelley, 1923.

and G are considered. Child A, according to parental report, did not begin using meaningful words until 36 months, while child G did not begin, according to parental report, until 24 months, and its I. Q. was 95, slightly below the average. It seems obvious that these two cases, as far as speech development is concerned, belong at an earlier place in the series, and are probably more nearly comparable to the higher percentages of Group I than with those of Group II. It would seem legitimate to exclude these in the computation, particularly with reference to the " self " pronouns, as it is in this series that such cases would tend to obscure the facts regarding the decrease in their use. Case E, the only other outstanding atypical case, has already been excluded when considering the " self " pronouns mainly for the reasons that its M.A. was below 33 and its percentage in connection with slow development was so disproportionate. As both of these other cases, A and G, are above 36 months, they were included in the main computations in spite of their slow development and exaggerated percentage. Later a few computations were performed excluding them for purposes of check against the figures already obtained.

A correlation for the 17 cases in this series was computed by the formula[1]

$$\eta yx = \frac{\sqrt{\dfrac{\Sigma nx \, (\bar{Y}_x - \bar{Y})^2}{N}}}{\sigma y}$$

The resulting coefficient for ηxy was $(-)$ ·858 and for ηyx was $(-)$ ·639 in contrast with a linear coefficient of $-$ ·636. ηyx is practically the same. Applying the correction for too fine groupings (Kelley, 1923, pp. 240–244) to ηxy reduces the coefficient to $(-)$ ·76. Applying the test for linearity (Kelley, 1923, p. 238) shows the difference not to be statistically significant. But for these cases under consideration the line of x on y does drop quite rapidly and then flatten out somewhat. However, we would have to test this out with other groups before it could be decided regarding the curvilinear character of the regression.

If the correlation is curvilinear instead of linear, it is

[1] η coefficients do not carry minus signs, but the positive or negative character may be determined by inspection.

difficult to know just what to attribute the curvilinear nature to. It may be due to the peculiarities of the sample. It may be that after a certain reduced percentage is obtained for the self pronouns, their use remains relatively constant. Thus they would probably cease to be an index of self integration. It might be due to the fact that the child's social situation is such that there is a plateau in development. It may also be that the number of words per minute, after a certain rate is reached, represents mere verbosity and does not indicate a corresponding symbolic integration. Thus it might follow that if we could get a truer measure of symbolic integration we should still find " self " references decreasing proportionately. However, all of these hypotheses must wait for further facts.

As a slight check on the above figures, the three atypical cases, E, A, and G, were excluded in computing ϵ, a Pearsonian frequency correlation and a curvilinear η_2 for the regression of x on y. The results are as follows : $M_1 -$ $M_2 = 2\cdot25 \pm \epsilon$ $1\cdot066$, showing greater statistical probability of significance. The $r = - \cdot667 \pm$ P.E. $\cdot096$, a slightly higher linear correlation. The $\eta_2 xy$ regression was $(-)$ $\cdot788$, somewhat lower than before. Cases A and G, when included, evidently exaggerated the fluctuation and enlarged the η_1 somewhat. The correlation for too fine groupings, however, should correct for this, and it did reduce the η_1 to $(-)$ $\cdot76$. This is quite close to the above η_2 which, from the appearance of the frequencies, does not require much in the way of correction for too fine groupings, as they are more uniformly bunched than before. The difference between the two η coefficients and the r still suggests that further facts should be obtained to decide whether the correlation is actually more curvilinear than linear.

The coefficients of correlation between the use of " you " (all forms) pronouns and average words per minute is positive, $+ \cdot855$. That between the " we " (all forms) pronouns and the same variable is practically the same, $+ \cdot85$.

This indicates that the line of symbolic social

H

development lies in expanding group and social integrations. Persons grow into group and wider relations. According to these data, symbolic development is at first centred around the self. This is naturally to be expected. The development is based upon the behaviour of the child in a small circle of face-to-face associations. The " you " persons are also closely associated with the " self ; " the different " you's " in the child's surroundings have their centre in the child's own "self." Greater symbolic integration brings more and more into play the " we " phases of group behaviour, which includes others with the self. This expansion goes on, the child becoming a member of different " we " groups. The third personal elements are also developing at the same time. The non-" we " groups, the "they" and "them," come into play as well. Evidently, the expansion of the personality and symbolic integration may go on until the child enters the larger universes of discourse where these more personal elements tend to be subordinated to non-personal symbolic behaviour. Also, symbolic development may come to a relative halt at innumerable points in between the self-centred stage and an impersonal universe of discourse.

Due to the small number of cases and the chance that a large deviating item might unduly influence the Pearsonian r, the Spearman rank order p was also computed. The p merely takes into consideration the rank of the items, thus eliminating the possibility of giving too much weight to a large deviation. These p coefficients were then translated into r coefficients by Pearson's correction. The results were practically the same with two exceptions. The correlation between the use of " self " pronouns and M.A. was raised from $-$ ·34 to $-$ ·57[1]. This also meant a change in the partial correlation coefficient of association between the Self Pronouns and the Average Words per minute with M.A. held constant. It was reduced from $-$ ·60 to $-$ ·515, which is still moderately high.

There is a hint in Mattson's data in comparison with

[1] This would tend to show that there is a real association and that the former low r was due to undue fluctuation in the data which tended to obscure the association.

those of Mrs. Horn (Table XX) that probably before the age of five years—Mrs. Horn's data are for kindergarten children, and the general age of such children is from four to six—there is a relative decrease in the " you "[1] along with a continued increase in the " we "[1] and third personal pronouns, but more comparative data are necessary in order to judge accurately the tendencies at these higher ages.   We cannot be sure that Horn's and Mattson's data are wholly comparable in this respect, although they probably do indicate the true tendency.

A summary of the frequency of the use of pronouns summarized from Mrs. Horn's and Miss Mattson's data is shown in footnote [2] (*see* also Tables XIV, XX).   In general, *the use of the personal pronouns follows the same order as the acquirement of these symbols* given in the last chapter. One should take into consideration the trends which appear in them at the older ages.   Thus, the conclusions drawn regarding the significance of the order of the acquirement of the personal pronominal symbols would be further

[1] All forms of this pronoun.
[2] The ranking in the use of the different pronouns is :—

For Mattson's data.	For Horn's data.
I—3,777	I—25,293
you—1,644	you—7,355
my—932	my—6,714
me—925	we—5,700
we—353	he—3,714
your—266	me—3,083
mine—230	they—2,921
us, them—189	she—2,317
he—153	them—2,122
she—141	mine—1,534
her—135	us—1,268
they—74	your—1,254
him—73	our—1,140
your—66	her—1,103
our—57	his—1,073
his—47	yours—1,002
myself—29	him—824
yourself—9	their—293
hers—7	myself—172
ours—4	ours—105
self, their—3	Includes no frequency
himself—2	below 41
herself, themselves—1	

When put in comparable terms of percentage the trends (*see* Table XX) show up more clearly.

emphasized by the similar order in the frequency of the use of them. In both Mattson's and Horn's data the *I* pronoun alone is over 1,000 above any other word in frequency. Of course the difference is greater with the lower ages.

TABLE XX.

COMPARISON OF THE USE OF THE PERSONAL PRONOUNS.[1]

Personal Pronouns Used.			Mattson's data. %	Horn's data. %
1st sing.	...	...	...	63·3	53·4
2nd person	...	...	...	21·3	13·9
3rd sing.	...	...	...	6·0	13·1
1st plural	...	...	...	6·5	11·9
3rd plural	...	...	...	2·9	7·8
Total	...	...		100·0	100·1

The facts in both of these chapters concerning the appearance and use of the personal, particularly the pronominal, symbols point to the importance of the development of the " self " and of " others " in symbolic integration. It points to the symbolic process as in essence a social process of personal and group interaction and interdependence.

[1] No word with a frequency below 41 is included. The inclusion of them should affect the percentages only slightly, on account of the large numbers and the fact that from an examination most of the pronoun, having a much larger frequency than 41, appear to be already included.

CHAPTER VIII

THE SYMBOLIC PROCESS AND DELAYED REACTION

FACTS were reviewed in Chapter III showing that apparently the most sound explanation of symbolic integration is that which bases it upon social conditioning and the interchange of social stimuli through the mechanisms of the social-vocal-auditory situation. The necessary mechanisms for the beginnings of symbols are given in this social-behaviour situation. This means that a study of symbolic development may be made through an observation of such social behaviour and that this process may be analysed in terms of behaviour. In the next four chapters an attempt was made to trace social-behaviour processes in the early symbolic development in children. Although in the past chapters the study of symbols has centred around the language symbols in general and spoken symbols in particular, symbolic behaviour is not limited to verbal language. When once symbols have arisen in behaviour, practically any act or object may become symbolic in character.

Another problem must be considered before taking up the question of symbolic integration and its relation to thinking. It is, are there symbolic mechanisms other than those which we have discussed which might perform the symbolic function in animals and children who cannot talk ? The question is not concerning those cases in which deaf-and-dumb have been taught to use symbols by those who already use language. It is a more fundamental problem than that ; namely, may there not be substitutive symbols independent of such language symbols and which function without necessary dependence upon social interaction and vocalization and the consequent language integration ?

This problem falls under the general category of substitute responses. Symbols are substitute responses for acts and objects, and function in behaviour in place of these acts and objects. Thus, the person can adjust to an absent situation by means of symbolic behaviour. Now if we take a problem situation and remove a certain simple but essential part, and the subject is still able to respond " as if " this essential part were present, it may be taken as evidence that the subject had in his behaviour processes substituted some response which serves the same function in his adjustment as did the part of the stimulus-situation which is now absent.

The most adequate technique which we have developed to test the existence of this type of substitution is the delayed-reaction experiment. In the delayed-reaction experiment an essential part (S) of the stimulus-situation is removed. If the subject can respond successfully " as if " the S were still there, we assume that it is able to substitute in some way another or possibly a symbolic S which defines the situation so that he can respond adequately to it. It would be equally legitimate to remove a part (R) of the response reaction in order to see whether the subject could substitute another R. At present, we are not able to remove the R as readily as we can the S.

Hunter's experiments (1913, 1917) in delayed reaction are the only substantial ones carried out with children. He also tested rats, dogs, and raccoons. Thus we get a comparison between children and other animals. Walton's experiment (1915) on the dog, and Köhler's on chimpanzees (1925), are also instructive in this connection.

The experiment of Hunter (1913) consisted in placing before the subject two or three similar entrances to compartments. The correct compartment was indicated by turning on an electric light at its entrance. If the subject selected the correct compartment, it would then be fed. After the subject was used to this proceeding, the light was turned off before the subject was allowed to respond. The length of time which the animal could wait after the light was gone and still make a correct response constituted the period of delay.

The results of his experiments are given in Table XXI. The rats and dogs were able to make a successful delay only when they maintained bodily orientation   Here the delay and response is obviously a function of bodily position and set; there is no necessity of introducing a substitute S in explaining their behaviour.   The raccoons and children, however, were able to respond correctly even though distraction took place and bodily orientation was lost.   In the latter case there is apparently a substitution of some kind for the absent stimulus at the time of the release.

TABLE XXI.

MAXIMUM AND MINIMUM DELAYED REACTION.

SOURCE : HUNTER, 1913.

Subject.			Minimum Delay.	Maximum Delay.
Rats	...	...	Either no learning or 3rd stage.[1]	10 sec.
Dogs	...	...	2 sec.	5 min.
Raccoons	...	...	3 sec.	25 sec.
Children	...	...	50 sec.	25 min.

The amount of delay for the raccoons, however, is much less than the minimum delay for children. But the minimum delay for children is much below the maximum for the children.   Table XXII shows the relation of age to the maximum delay.   The raccoons and 2½-year-old child are much closer together.

TABLE XXII.

MAXIMUM DELAY FOR RACCOONS AND CHILDREN.

SOURCE : HUNTER, 1913.

Subject.				Maximum Delay.
Raccoons	...	...	...	25 sec.
2½-year-old child	...	...	...	50 sec.
6–8-year children	...	...	...	25 min. or more.

Hunter concludes that there is a type of response which he calls " sensory thought," involving the reinstatement of a recent sensory process but not requiring ideas or

[1] The 3rd stage was shutting off light at time of release from release box.

"images." The raccoons and younger child illustrate this. But a second type of thought requires ideas or images. The older children illustrate the latter.

Before we examine these conclusions, it might be well to refer to the other delayed-reaction experiments mentioned above. Walton tried a larger variety of experiments on the dog and found it able to delay reaction one minute without the aid of bodily orientation. This is for a longer period than for either the raccoons or the $2\frac{1}{2}$-year-old child. Köhler tried burying fruit so that the chimpanzees could see the proceedings (1925, p. 290 *ff*). Sultan, after half an hour, succeeded in digging up the fruit at the first attempt. A second time, after one hour, he dug 30 centimetres off, then succeeded on the second attempt. Another time the fruit was buried in the lot at night with the apes watching. Next morning, after $16\frac{1}{2}$ hours, they went to the right spot (several control spots had been dug and covered in the meantime) 60 centimetres off. The second attempt was successful. Another time, after $16\frac{1}{2}$ hours, they went straight to the spot in the morning. Sufficient controls were not established to make these experiments by Köhler wholly comparable with the other experiments on delayed reaction. It is not certain that the stimulus at the end of the delay was not the same as it was in the final form at the beginning ; thus the present stimulus would be sufficient to produce a correct response without involving the reproduction of an absent one. This seems somewhat comparable to the situation in which any animal returns to the place where it has been stimulated by food at some previous time. Köhler feels that the experiments should be carried out under more controlled conditions. However, it is suggestive of a type of response, possibly as complex as those of the raccoons, the child, and Walton's dog. But it hardly seems necessary to call symbols to our aid in explaining this behaviour of the apes. Engramic principles and learning are apparently sufficient to account for such behaviour without the aid of symbols. A problem more applicable for testing the use of symbols is that involving the use of tools. In regard to this Köhler says (1925, p. 25), " The best tool easily loses its situational value if it is not visible simultaneously or quasi-simultaneously with the region of the objective." This indicates the difficulty which the ape has in not being able to substitute a symbol for the tool when absent. It is probable that we need a but little, if any, more complex form of integration to explain the behaviour of apes than we do to explain that of the young child and the dog.

Hunter somewhat later (1917) tried an experiment on a younger child, T, from 13 to 16 months of age. His object was to take the child before true vocal language had developed. This child was evidently in the " parrot stage," without true vocal symbols. When its father was away and the door made a noise, it would sometimes say " Daddy." It said " boob-boob " for dog, " y-gob, y-gob " for turkey, and the like. Instead of light and food, Hunter used three similar boxes in which a toy could be concealed while the child was looking. After delay the child was to select the right box in order to find its toy. In the meantime the child was distracted in some manner. This was apparently very interesting sport for the child. Hunter's results are as follows : At December 2nd, ten seconds may be considered mastered. At January 10th, the 20-second interval may be considered as being approximately mastered. (*See* Table XXIII.)

The real situation seems to be more favourable than this for both dates ; for instance, on November 12th, he was correct seven out of ten times at 20 seconds' or more delay. Problems of fatigue and motivation are such as to have a tendency to underrate the child in such an experiment.

Hunter says that it is probable that the 2½-year-old child, F, in the earlier experiment, would have been more successful under the conditions used for T. His delay would probably have been substantially longer.

A summary of the results regarding those cases which possibly involve some sort of substitution gives :

Maximum Delay.

1. { The 13–16-months child   ..   .. 20 seconds or more.
   { Raccoons   ..   ..   .. 25 seconds.

2. { The 2½-year child   ..   .. 50 seconds (would probably have more with Hunter's second technique).
   { The dog—Walton   ..   .. 1 minute.

3. The 6–8-year-old children   .. 25 minutes or more.

By placing the results of these three experiments together, it is not intended to indicate that they are strictly comparable in the amount of delay for the different experiments. Some of the varying factors have already been indicated. However, the comparison is sufficiently close to give evidence of the two types of response as well as of continuity between children and other animals in this respect.

TABLE XXIII.

THE DELAYED REACTION OF HUNTER'S CHILD, AGE 13 TO 16 MONTHS, HAVING NO TRUE VOCAL LANGUAGE.

SOURCE : HUNTER, 1917.

Last part of Oct. and Nov. through Dec. 2nd.

Delays.						% Correct.
3–7 sec.	...	...	...	...	...	... 88
8–12 sec.	...	...	...	...	...	... 72
13–17 sec.	...	...	...	...	...	... 55
18–22 sec.	...	...	...	...	...	... 37
23–35 sec.	...	...	...	...	...	... 44

Ten-sec. interval may be considered mastered.

Jan. 2nd—Jan. 10th.

5–7 sec. ...	...	...	...	...	...	... 77
8–12 sec. ...	...	...	...	...	...	... 82
15 sec. ...	...	...	...	...	...	... 75
20 sec. ...	...	...	...	...	...	... 70
25 sec. ...	...	...	...	...	...	... 50

Twenty-sec. interval may be considered as approximately mastered.

The type of substitution in 1 and 2 probably represents different degrees of a similar substitution—what Hunter calls " sensory thought."

What seems to happen in these cases is that there are relatively temporary and plastic residual responses to the absent stimulus. When the situation minus the stimulus again is presented, these residual responses occur or are occurring, and are adequate substitutes for the original but absent part, They constitute a plastic or temporary tendency to respond with reference to the total situation in a particular fashion due to a previous particular stimulus. In the light of the Gestalt findings it may be that a temporary configuration is established and the stimulus still remains adequate for a correct response due to its " form " value, and in spite of the fact that a part of the stimulus is absent. Although Hunter thinks that the possibility of an after-image is not involved, still there may be some sort of motor change or after-effect, possibly engramic, which carries over directly to the end of the successful delay. In any case, the ability to respond correctly is very limited regarding the amount of delay, and represents a much lower degree in comparison with the older children.

This complex mechanism of response, however, is evidently material out of which symbols are made, but it is evidently not the type of behaviour called symbolic in the sense in which the substitute is performed accompanied by the associated behaviour which sets it off as a definition of the stimulus and response. The small amount of delay indicates that the substitution is apparently a rather direct function of the original stimulus. Removal of the original stimulus-situation for longer than a very short period makes successful response a matter of chance. Whereas the true symbolic substitution after being initiated by the original stimulus-situation becomes relatively independent of it and becomes substitutive as a function of the stimulus-situation-minus-S. The symbol is no longer immediately dependent upon the original stimulus-situation, but now defines the stimulus-situation-minus-S and makes possible a correct response to it when it is presented after a long delay.

Symbolic integration thus involves a more complicated

behaviour pattern.   It represents a much more unitary organization of behaviour than that represented by the short delay.

There is no sharp dividing line, however, between these two kinds of substitutive action, nor no sharp one between the more simple and the complex conditioned responses. The child in infancy is apparently on the same footing as other so-called higher animals.   He is capable of becoming more complexly conditioned and integrated, but does not represent a form *sui generis* in the animal world.   The degree of difference subsequently obtained is substantial. It is probable that a great deal of the adjustment of humans goes on in the realm of the short delayed reaction which may be classified as belonging to sub-symbolic processes.

Now to return to the main question with which we started.   It seems true from these and other data that, as far as is known, the symbolic type of behaviour develops only with the social-vocal beginnings.   The child of $2\frac{1}{2}$ who delayed only 50 seconds probably represents a case where the experimental situation was not so well adapted to the child's stage of development as it might have been. As Hunter states, under conditions similar to those of T, his delay would probably have been substantially longer. Walton's situation probably was quite favourable for the dog, as it should be, due to its previous habits, such as food-getting and the like.   Thus under more favourable experimental conditions for the $2\frac{1}{2}$-year child, who had already begun to use true vocal language, his period of delay might have been considerably more than that of the dog.   However, we should not expect a very great amount of delay at the stage of integration obtained by a $2\frac{1}{2}$-year-old child.

For the present, the point of emphasis is merely that the social-vocal behaviour situation apparently furnishes the requisite mechanisms for true symbolic integration when associated with a sufficiently complex-behaviour system.   And up to the present, this social-behaviour situation is the only situation in which such a type of behaviour has occurred. It is true, of course, that with the use of similar principles, language has been developed in the deaf-and-dumb, but by highly mechanical and artificial manipulation and by those who already have developed language by means of the vocal integration. Symbolic integration will be considered in the following chapter.

CHAPTER IX

THE NATURE OF SYMBOLIC INTEGRATION

HAVING analysed materials indicating the important part played by social behaviour in symbolic development, it will now be valuable to bring these facts together again into a more specific statement regarding the nature of symbolic integration, giving these social factors a clearer and more balanced place in the explanation. Three main conceptions are included in the term "integration." The first is the dynamic or change-aspect involved in the coming together or the emergence of a new or different organization, co-ordination, or configuration. The second is the continuity and causal aspect, in that the emergence is from or out of previously existing correlations and processes and is dependent upon these. The third is the unitary aspect, *i.e.*, the emergent or configuration constitutes some sort of a functional unit or working whole. A co-ordination and division of labour are indicative of this aspect. The problem is simply one of indicating previous processes, and of explaining how the new organization is created and of discovering what sort of functional unit or emergent it is.

From our previous analysis it is clear that we may come to grips with the problem in the general field of social interaction and more specifically in the "complex social act," to use Mead's apt phrase. The complex social act consists of the operation of interdependent behaviour systems. It will thus be convenient, even though somewhat artificial, to take for a time the individual as a point of reference from which to observe the operation of complex social behaviour involved in the integration of symbols. That such a procedure may be quite artificial if not handled carefully is clear when it is recalled that such social activity cannot exist in separate and isolated individuals, but only in their interdependence. The attempt to actually separate persons would be somewhat analogous to the much simpler procedure of extracting the Na from the Cl in salt. Part of the result, if used properly, might be beneficial for a cold in the head, but it would hardly be used to season soup. And while studying so-called individual behaviour systems, it must be clearly kept in mind that they are not to be regarded as separate units, but as phases of social behaviour.

That the total act must be regarded as a whole, something more than a summation of parts, has been well and convincingly emphasized by the Gestalt psychologists, among others. So that the problem is not so much one of tearing the symbolic process to pieces as one might a watch and then pointing to the pieces as a description of a watch, as it is of discovering the processes at work which are involved in the emergence of symbols in behaviour.

Before going into the problem more specifically, it seems necessary to point out certain characteristics of symbols which must be taken into consideration. The symbol involves the use by the organism of some act or sign which is differentiated from, but at the same time is a substitute for, an act or object. It is necessary to emphasize this point in order to show the inadequacy of an explanation of symbolic origin which is apt to appear valid upon casual examination, but which really does not give the necessary facts with which to account for the origin of symbols. The theory runs somewhat as follows : It assumes that symbols might have arisen through gestures, perhaps facial or hand gestures. Suppose two apes attempt to eat an extremely pungent fruit and make facial contortions of disgust. Thus, mutually observing each other, this particular grimace gets to symbolize a disgust of distasteful fruit. Such behaviour, however, is inadequate to account for the development of a symbol. First, we must differentiate between signs and symbols. The sign is an event which, due to its association with some other event or object, signalizes the latter. There is a large group of stimuli which function in this manner. The danger calls and the sex calls of animals are examples. The hen's pecking is a sign to the chick to peck. Of course, it is clear that these signs are not objects of reflection for these animals. It is only to animals with symbols that these signs become objects of reflection. For other animals they exist as stimuli, often conditioned stimuli which arouse responses. Just as in the case of Clever Hans, for example, the reaction of the audience when he had counted the proper number, was a sign, or conditioned stimulus for him to stop. These aspects of conditioned and unconditioned response are so familiar that no more need be added to show how clearly they can account for gesture signs without implying symbolic reference.

It is undoubtedly true that signs are prior to and form an easy framework for the development of symbols. Ogden and Richards (1923) have very convincingly discussed the fundamental· characteristics of the sign-situation.

What is lacking in the above gesture situation is this, the ape by his behaviour does not set off the grimace or gesture as separate from, but symbolizing the bitter fruit. He responds to both on their own account as stimuli. The ape does not stimulate himself with the gesture and react to it as representing a bitter object. In order for him to do this, there would have to be more similarity— enough, in fact, for his own stimulus to stimulate himself just as the other ape's gesture does. He cannot see his own grimace, or if it were a gesture, it would not appear to him as similar to the other ape's gesture, and consequently, could not be substituted for or symbolize the gesture of the other ape ; much less could it symbolize the fruit. He reacts to the other's stimulus as a conditioned stimulus, not as a stimulus representing the bitter object. What would be necessary in order to complete the symbol from the sign is that the ape should be able to stimulate himself with a stimulus so similar to the gesture of the other ape that he would arouse responses to his own act setting it off as different from the other, and at the same time arousing the responses which differentiate the act as that of the other, thus dividing the behaviour system into two reacting parts which give the symbol its symbolic character. The social-vocal-auditory situation makes this possible. It may be due to the peculiarities of bodily structure that it is the vocal response which is thus interchangeable, and certainly any other such consistently interchangeable stimulus might also perform this function in animals with a sufficiently developed nervous system, but so far as we know there are no other such stimuli, except the vocal responses, that existed before vocal language developed in social behaviour. Of course, after symbols were once integrated, it became possible to produce similar interchangeable characteristics in other stimuli than the vocal ones. In any case the social situation remains a prime essential.

It is due to this method of developing symbols that all our symbols are acquired indirectly. But the significance of this point will be taken up later, as it can hardly be overemphasized.

As some of the aspects of conditioned response in relation to symbolic integration have already been discussed in Chapter III, the problem may again be taken up at this point.

In résumé, the situation is somewhat as follows. The S-R (stimulus-response) relationship functions in a biological or organic process. With the life process, as observed in less complex organisms, and to a large degree in man, scientists have demonstrated balanced functional (mathematically speaking) relationships. Psychologically, we may state it in the elementary formula RfS or SfR. From this we may proceed to the more specific aspect involving the symbolic process.

The symbolic process is the use of a substitute stimulus or response for the elementary terms in this equation. Not all substitution of S or R is symbolic. There is the

I

more simple-conditioned response type of substitution which may be put in a formula as follows :

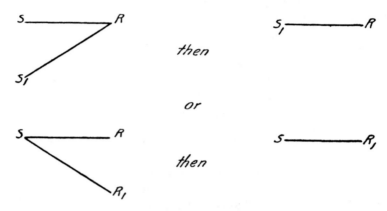

There is reason to believe that this conditioning process may go on to a rather refined degree where S_2 is substituted for S_1, S_3 for S_2, etc., and similarly for R. The degree of conditioning would vary with different types of response, but there are limitations. We could hardly expect to get a person conditioned to enjoy strenuous electric shocks.

The type of substitution in the symbolic behaviour is one in which a third factor is introduced by more complex conditioning and remains as a substitute for the S and R, as shown in the figure.

The essential difference is that in the previous type of substitution the S defines the R and the R defines the S. They are defined in terms of each other, whereas the SR defines the S and R in a third term including processes of both S and R. The functional relationship still maintains.

At this point certain qualifications must be made regarding the conditioned response. No such thing exists in the isolated manner in which it is juggled about by some psychologists. Neither stimuli nor responses exist separately. These are merely devices for observing and measuring behaviour and after use must be thrown back into the dynamics of behaviour units and wholes. Too often they give little inkling of how the whole actually performs or what it is. If this process of conditioning responses is thought of as one in which one figure is merely replaced by another as in a simple algebraic formula, or as a mere summation of parts, such a conception must be discarded. And if the concept of conditioned response carries only this theory, it must also follow to the same scrap heap. Some psychologists, in their attempt to place psychology upon a sound scientific basis, have oversimplified psychological processes by making such phenomena as conditioning a matter of the simple substitution of one response or stimulus for another, as one might substitute lettuce for onions at a meal.

It seems that a good share of the argument centring around mechanism, vitalism and the like resolves itself into such oversimplification, or if the oversimplification is not intended it is imputed and the consequent attack is as violent as if the straw figure were a real one. Of course, in addition to all these unduly simplified explanations are a whole list of conjurations which add unwarranted complexity, mystification, and confusion to psychological description.

In view of this state of affairs it seems advisable that this problem of the mechanistic or non-mechanistic character of behaviour processes should be tackled at once in order to properly clarify the following discussion.

Some have regarded mechanistic, when applied to behaviour processes, as involving a static condition such as is found in a machine. Everything that the machine can do already exists in its organization. The thing is made and stays put—nothing new develops in its operation. Thus the term mechanistic has implied a form of contact such as seen in the contact of the cogs of a gear wheel, and not as the contact of an electric spark with a high explosive,

for instance.   They have tended to treat mechanistic as
meaning mere contact without the realization that there
is no such thing as contact abstracted from what takes
place when contact occurs.   They have neglected to look
at contact as initiating interaction.   Mechanistic has been
regarded as indicative of a mere additive or a simple
multiplication process.   However, it is setting up something of a straw man to say in general that those who
attempt a mechanistic explanation of behaviour intend
to use the term in such a limited sense.   By numerous
writers it is merely used to indicate a dependent or sequential relationship, sometimes called a causal relationship,
and nothing more.   The term " mechanistic " is sometimes
preferable to " causal " on account of the fact that we are not
sure what actually " causes " phenomena to occur.   Scien-
tifically, it cannot be said with certainty that one event
causes another.   We merely know inductively that certain
events always occur together or in sequence, in a functional
relationship.   Thus the term " cause " is apt to carry a mythical content which " mechanistic " does not do.   Further,
mechanistic when used in psychology is apt to mean the
implication of a physical and chemical basis for life and
behaviour processes.   Now, while this cannot be proven
for a large number of phenomena, it has such a preponderance of scientific evidence behind it that it is a justified
hypothesis until it is proven inadequate, not merely by
showing processes still unexplained, but by showing
contrary facts.

Mechanistic, then, when used with the idea of a dependent functional relationship, can hardly have objections
brought against it on this score by the scientific man.
When it is also regarded as an hypothesis which assumes
a physical and chemical basis for life and behaviour
processes, it may be open to more serious objection in the
minds of some.   However, such an hypothesis can scarcely
be rejected as a working basis in biology and psychology
until its opponents have demonstrated on scientific grounds
its inadequacy.

Thus, when mechanistic is used here, it carries these

two implications : the existence of dependent functional relationships, and the hypothesis of a physical and chemical basis for life and behaviour processes. It does not imply that new wholes and new configurations, *i.e.*, invention or creation and discovery, are not facts of science, nor does it imply that we necessarily find these new integrations in isolated parts or their mere summation.

With this conception clarified, the discussion may return to the conditioned response.

It is probable that the conditioned response conception cannot be relied upon to give an adequate idea of symbolic integration on account of its encumbrance with such a conception as mathematical substitution instead of mathematical multiplication and even more complex dependence. By a more complex dependence is meant such a situation, for example, as is given when different chemical substances result in a third which is more than the mere addition of $1 + 2$. Behaviour integrations are apparently often much more complex than this.

In going beyond or behind the conditioned response conception, there is no intention of regarding it as invalid when properly understood and used. Conditioning is, on the contrary, a demonstrable fact, and plays an important part in symbolic integration, as already indicated. The following analysis should put more content into it.

As hinted before, we do not know the " real nature " of what happens in irritable cells, particularly nerve cells, upon stimulation any more than we know the " real nature" of electricity. Our greatest advance has been in describing and explaining their activity and behaviour, in showing the physical, chemical or electrical aspect of their processes, in formulating laws, and in establishing theories and hypotheses which most adequately account for the observed facts.

It would take the present study too far out of its present limits to go into all this material, relating to physiological and behaviour processes, in order to give an adequate idea of the complex behaviour systems which form an integral part of symbolic integration. The writings of such scientists as Child, Herrick, Loeb, Jennings, Sherrington, Lashley, Semon, Pavlov, Cannon, and many others are mines of physiological and behaviouristic information regarding these phenomena.   Only some brief points may be emphasized.

The organism is some sort of energetic system with excitation-irritability characteristics. As a result of stimulation and excitation, material changes or traces are left in the cells of the body.   Semon has used the term engram—" an enduring material change of the irritable substance " which remains behind and, though latent, " can be roused to manifestation at any moment in conformity with known laws " (1921, p. 273)—to designate this result.   The rearousal of the mnemic trace or engram from its latent state he calls ecphory (1921, p. 12). Engramic effects are distinct from each other, but all of those stimuli occurring simultaneously leave behind engrams in juxtaposition which are coherently associated ; i.e., an engramic complex.   Engrams also successively tie into each other in a continuous unilinear manner.   Each separate stimulus, although of the same kind, leaves its separate engram.   In using the term " engram " there is no intention of subscribing to a too structural conception of such physiological changes.   These physiological changes which are left and facilitate a subsequent rearousal and reoccurrence of responses is all that is intended by the use of the term.   The continuous change and reshaping which goes on in behaviour patterns, their non-specific character, is well emphasized by Child (1924).   This work should be read as an antidote to a too structural conception of engramic changes.

Thus any of the more differentiated organisms represent very intricate organization of engramic complexes.   Child and Herrick have shown how the more irritable parts of the cell dominate by gradients over the rest of the cell, and also that the more irritable cells and parts of the body establish excitation-gradients over the rest.   Such central dominance over engramic complexes gives the organism a remarkable ability of response and adjustment in co-ordinating ecphorized engramic or mnemic excitation with present original stimulation.

These processes occur among all organisms and it should be emphasized that activity which is non-symbolic is often very complex and highly integrated. This latter point is particularly important, for when these processes occur among other animals they are accepted under causal rubrics, but when they appear in man they are often treated as though they had taken on a mysterious something which defies causal analysis. While it is very essential that these processes be explained on their own account, they are for the present accepted as given; the problem is to explain the additional integration involved in the development of symbols. It is probably much more difficult to explain the ordinary complex activity of so-called higher animals than given this to show the further integration resulting in symbolic emergents.

These complex behaviour systems exist only in social groupings of some sort. This fact makes possible a much more intricate organization of behaviour. Individual behaviour systems are not independent, but become in our more complex grouping mere " truncated acts," the complete or " whole " process existing only in the group and not in the individual as such. In this sense it is legitimate to speak of a group unity and proceed to analyse the group behaviour as a group process and not as a bunch of separate individuals. This, of course, must not be taken to mean that this group exists separate or apart from individuals, it is an interrelation of individuals. It is in such social situations and behaviour systems that symbolic integration occurs.

Figures B, C and D are given as suggestive of symbolic integration. They give a simple representation of a complex social act in which the hungry child reacts vocally, the mother comes with food, also responding vocally, and the child is fed. Figure B shows the complex social act as it might exist with slight modifications in a more or less complicated form in a large number of different animal groups. This may represent pre-symbolic behaviour on the part of both organisms involved, if we assume M_1 and M_2 to be mere vocalizations. As a basis for symbolic integration, it would be necessary for these vocalizations to be sufficiently similar to be interchanged, as is seen in children's behaviour, and which undoubtedly marked

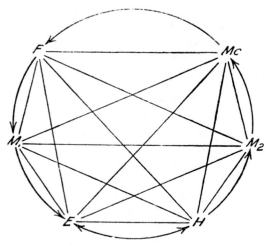

H —Hunger Reactions.
M_2—Child's verbal response Ma or Mik, etc.
Mc—Mother comes.
F —Food.
M_1—Mother's verbal stimulus Ma or Mik, etc.
E —Child is fed.
Lines—Mnemic connections in the child's behaviour.

The child's own verbal response becomes conditioned to and substitutive for other parts of the complex act.

FIG. B.—THE COMPLEX SOCIAL ACT.

symbolic beginning in the race as well. The interconnecting lines represent the interconnections of the act in the child's behaviour system. They represent engrams or physiological modifications in juxtaposition, forming a whole engramic-complex of mnemic traces which may be ecphorized by any one of the associated or conditioned stimuli as well as by certain states of organic excitement.[1]

[1] Some may find Hollingworth's conception of "redintegration" helpful in this connection. The general formula is in "that type of learning in which a partial detail, as C, of a complex event, ABCDE, touches off a complete response, XYZ, which formerly . . . was touched off only by the complete event ABCDE" (1926, p. x, 222).

Figure C represents more explicitly the child's present original responses associated with ecphorized mnemic excitation of engramic-complexes. During the child's babbling period repetition after repetition of such stimulation occurs. Similar mnemic revival occurs together with present original stimulation and the two interact, adjust and strengthen each other (*see* an explanation of homophony by Semon, 1921).

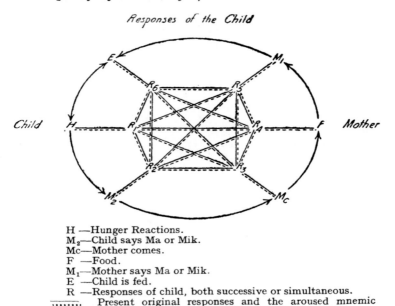

Responses of the Child

H —Hunger Reactions.
M_2—Child says Ma or Mik.
Mc—Mother comes.
F —Food.
M_1—Mother says Ma or Mik.
E —Child is fed.
R —Responses of child, both successive or simultaneous.
....   Present original responses and the aroused mnemic engram-complexes.

Fig. C.—The Child's Responses in Relation to the Mother's Acts in the Complex Social Act.

Figure D illustrates the integration of the symbol when the child's vocal response has been interchanged with that of the mother. The child thus arouses its engramic and original present responses to its mother, but also arouses its engramic and original present responses to itself. Such behaviour processes as facilitation, irradiation, more than mere additive summation and gradiential domination, are very significant aspects of such behaviour.

The child performs his own part of the complex act and at the same time performs another's part as well. The engramic arousal and beginning responses of the child toward the mother's stimulus for which its vocal response has been substituted, are thus directed toward another part of its own behaviour mechanisms consisting of further engramic and original present responses. These two configurations or parts of behaviour, from their simultaneous

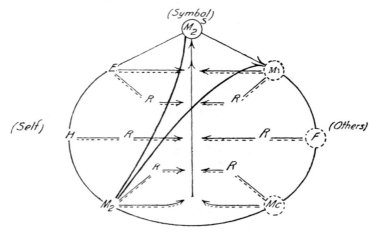

FIG. D.—THE SYMBOLIC CONFIGURATION.

AN ANALYSIS OF THE COMPLEX SOCIAL ACT—THE " SYMBOL," THE
" SELF," AND " OTHERS."

Hunger reactions (H) occur, the child says Ma-Ma (M_2) so similar to this word said by its mother (M_1) that it represents the mother's word by arousing the mnemic responses to the acts of the mother along with other responses to its own voice (M_2) as such. A whole of engramic-complexes is ecphorized. The child's engramic responses are turned upon its own stimulus as well as upon other of its own engramic responses. Thus within the child's behaviour system are two sets of responses (" Other " and " Self ") reacting toward each other specifically and involving the parts of the complex social act. The vocal stimulus emerges from this behaviour analysis as a symbol which designates the " self " and the " other," and as a symbol which designates and defines by behaviour reactions specific situations.

··········· Represents original and engramic responses. Some of the complex interconnections are not shown for sake of greater simplicity.

interaction serve to mark off, or analyse, the parts of the complex social act. The interchanged stimulus is thus designated by behaviour reactions as representing, while still distinct from, the mother's part of the social act. It is also similarly representative of the child's own behaviour. This constitutes it as a symbol. It is thus that the stimulus which arouses the "self" and "other" aspects of behaviour, emerges as a symbol of these parts and as a behaviour analysis of the situation. This process, by which symbols emerge and operate, is what is meant by the symbolic process. It should also be remembered that emotional responses of the child are very important in symbolic integration. Practically all responses either are or become more or less emotional in character. The situation, including parental or similar associations, in which the child lives, is ordinarily one of strong emotional interaction and conditioning. Much more study of emotional responses is necessary, but sufficient is known regarding them to testify to their outstanding importance in motivating activity and also in the fixation and conditioning of responses. Thus the extensive rôle played by emotional responses in symbolic integration is one of greatly facilitating such development.

Symbols at first are apparently used for all similar situations to which they may apply, and to designate the whole event. It is only by further social interaction that symbols are disintegrated and new ones integrated or redintegrated to designate more specific parts of the act or situation.

The validity of the symbol depends upon the complex act. Particularly must the specific part interchanged, *i.e.*, the vocalization, be consistently configurated and conditioned with the act by the behaviour mechanisms of both persons ; otherwise it would have such an insecure place in the co-ordination that it would neither serve as a symbol nor as a means of interchange. If the complex social act or object becomes changed or modified so that it is no longer sufficiently consistent with the symbolic configuration, the symbolic character of the configuration is destroyed. The result is that a new symbol must be integrated which does answer consistently to the parts of the act. These are essential characteristics of it as a symbol, and mean that the symbol is essentially a social and common product dependent in the final analysis upon its social character.

Just what a symbol and its content will be cannot be predicted beforehand, for it is yet in process of construction. For the individuals concerned to know ahead of time or before the symbol is integrated what it is to be is a contradiction of terms.

From this standpoint the symbolic process can never be catalogued as mechanistic, if by such a term is meant machine-like addition or summation. It is essentially inventive or creative in operation. The fact that the content of the symbol is unpredictable until it is once integrated has reference primarily to its first genesis. But even before a symbol has ever existed, some of the content is predictable in a limited sense, if previous symbols by their nature must form some of the phases of the new symbol. After the symbol once emerges, it may then be explained mechanistically in a causal sense with the presupposition of a chemical and physical basis. And other similar symbols may be produced or predicted under similar conditions. That is, while the specific symbolic configuration may be unpredictable until known, still its integration is to be explained causally and as involving a functional relationship. And given a knowledge of and acquaintance with a person, a social psychologist can often predict the symbolic configuration which will result from a new problem presented to a subject, and certainly so if he knows all the factors which will come into consideration. We know, for instance, that under certain social conditions a bright, energetic boy will develop a symbol of himself as the " bad boy " of the neighbourhood.

Also laws of the operation of the symbolic process may be generalized just as we generalize chemical laws. But new and unforeseen symbolic integrations such as inventions occur, just as new chemical integrations occur. And it seems quite likely that when we know as much about the laws of the symbolic process as we do about chemical laws we shall be able to make similarly remarkable symbolic integrations and inventions.

The " self " and " other " phases of symbolic integration have already been briefly discussed (Chapters V, VI) and will receive attention later.   The fundamental characteristic of this social aspect is one which can hardly be overemphasized, due to the fact of the neglect of it even in most recent and outstanding studies of symbolic development. It is not so much that the social phase is intentionally ignored as that it is unwittingly neglected, the investigator assuming that it has been adequately treated, or that it is beyond the limits of his study.   This latter is a prevalent reason for overlooking the integral social character of symbolic integration.   In general, studies do not attempt to trace the actual genesis of symbols.   They assume the existence of symbols and describe later development.

It is well to emphasize again that this explanation has not called upon some mysterious " psychic " or the like, but has been an attempt to explain symbolic integration in terms of the social behaviour of organisms.   As a basis, living physiological organisms with their physiological foundations of behaviour as disclosed by neurological and behaviouristic study were all that was assumed.   With such organisms as a basis, the social vocal-auditory situation has been used to give an account of the development of symbols.   It is true that this is not a complete explanation—nothing has ever been " completely " explained. "Life" has not been explained in the above analysis, and this is what a large number of people want when an attempt is made to explain such symbolic phenomena.   But it was not our task to explain life.   Life processes were assumed and within such a biological process the difference between non-symbolic behaviour and symbolic behaviour appears to be a matter of the social interaction which has been described.   The life process is apparently continuous from the most simple to the most complex.   It is the forms and types of interaction in association with the complexity which give us the most adequate account of symbolic integration rather than the bringing in of a new element which is a mystery and remains unexplained. Even though such a mystery as " psychic " were verbally introduced, it would be something which would still require analysis and explanation, and in doing this we should apparently be forced back upon some such behaviouristic analysis as already given, which, although incomplete, goes farther than merely using a name for a mystery. There is plenty of room for mystery in other places. We do not need to foster ignorance to perpetuate such enjoyment.

In view of the fact that most investigators assume a very fundamental relation between symbolic behaviour and thinking, and treat them accordingly, this aspect, along with the further investigation into the social character, the " self " and other " personal " phases of the symbolic process, will be discussed in the following chapter on the subject of the self and reflective (thinking) behaviour. Up to this point we have left such terms as " meaning " and the like out of the explanation. The problem of the next chapter is to see how far this sort of behaviouristic description will account for " thinking."

CHAPTER X

IT seems rather dangerous to attempt to define such a term as "thinking." It appears to be a catch-all of so many things regarding which we are ignorant or confused, a depository for unexplained odds and ends of behaviour, second perhaps to the word consciousness in ambiguity, for thinking is added unto the sins of consciousness. However, the process which would include "thinking" must be that during mediate response, in the field of excitation when the ordinary routine and otherwise balanced stimulus response situations or wholes fail to function. There are a large number of behaviour processes which are characterized by immediate and adequate response to stimuli, in which there is no place in the causal sequence for the phenomena called "thinking." The equilibrium established by this immediate type of response is accounted for without the assumption of such an intermediate process. Thinking is a function of mediate response—stating the proposition in very general terms. Without any further explanation of thinking at this point, the mediate response cue will be followed.

In animals other than man, psychologists account in general for the processes occurring during a period of excitation and mediate response without assuming so-called reflective or ideational thinking.[1]

In experiments on animal behaviour a disturbing stimulus is provided in connection with a problem to be solved before an adequate response can be completed.

---

[1] See Herrick, 1926, Ch. XIII, for a good short summary. It should be noted that he somewhat overstates (pp. 24 f) the significance of Köhler's experiments on apes. (See Köhler, 1925, pp. 53 ff, 276 f.)

Thus the adjustment or problem solving behaviour can be observed. So thoroughly has this been studied by psychologists and neurologists that it can be explained quite well upon the basis of the organic responses which occur, the activity of muscles and glands, bio-physical and bio-chemical processes, engramic effects and the like. A great deal of this behaviour is directly observable in overt response or by instruments. A simple illustration— many others might be used—will bring out some of the important elements for present purposes.

A dog, for example, is presented with a situation in which he must jump an obstacle, a fence, in order to obtain food. His responses to this obstacle define it for him. He may run along the fence, may smell along the edges, step up on to the vertical surface, try to push through to the food, and finally jump over. An analysis of the fence is here accomplished by the responses of the dog. Into this set of responses, which results in an analysis of the fence-obstacles, will enter past habits, muscular " memory," ecphorized engrams, conditioned responses, or in short, the whole behaviour mechanism with its past experiences. The meaning of the obstacle for the dog (not that he " reflects " or " thinks " about it) is given in this complex of responses, they define the obstacle. It is something which he jumps over in order to reach the food. In a causal or mechanistic explanation of behaviour, this is the only place to look for meaning. The meaning of the stimulus is to be found in the total complex of responses to it.

It might also be pointed out that between the initial food stimulus and the final response of eating, what goes on is a series of immediate responses to stimuli and organic influences. This is one fact which makes possible an explanation not involving thinking. There are, of course, some responses which take a relatively long period to complete, but, in general, they are to be explained in a similar manner. However, there are borderline cases.

Köhler, in his stimulating book, *The Mentality of Apes*, gives instances where the ape stopped random and useless activity, surveyed the situation or scratched the head, then immediately executed a correct solution of the problem. He says that this pause is striking in contrast to other behaviour. He concludes that the ape acts with "insight" (*Einsicht*). Anyone reading through his experiment with an unbiased attitude must agree that he presents facts which justify him in distinguishing this type of activity—whether it is called insight or by another name is not as important as the specific facts described. Here there is a type of mediate behaviour in which some sort of integration evidently occurs which enables the ape to correctly solve his problem. The act of integration is made possible, or at least facilitated, by the pause. In such a mediate response there is a clear break which must be accounted for. Another example of a mediate type of response is that already described in the delayed reactions of raccoons, the dog, and young children.

If it would add anything to our knowledge of what takes place in the ape's behaviour during this period of " insight," it would be justifiable, it seems, to call it some kind of thinking. Similarly, the mutual interaction of different behaviour patterns of the ape might be called reasoning, in that there is evidently some sort of reaction towards consistency occurring in the ape's behaviour among the complex of responses, including those already acquired for responding to less complicated problems. The dog's analysis of the obstacle, described above, by more active responses is not greatly different, although simpler. However, these terms add little to our knowledge of what happens. Insight does poorly enough as a pointer. Or, to call such activity " sensory thought," as Hunter does for the short delayed reactions, seems to add little to our knowledge of what takes place. At best " sensational psychology " gives us little enough information regarding what happens in the limited phase of psychology to which it may be pertinent. A more fruitful line of investigation is that of determining more exactly what sort of action goes on rather than positing supposed " sensory elements " which themselves remain unexplained.

K

This is not to decry anything which a study of qualities, feelings, so-called sensations, and the like, may contribute to our understanding of behaviour. But it does emphasize the necessity of going much further than these terms take us. If they are accepted at all their rôle is apparently that of pointers to a problem and not the basis for analysis.

Approaching an explanation of such activity from the standpoint of the behaviour involved, it is possible to come to a clearer understanding of the nature of it. Concerning this type of activity in the apes, the situation is such that the ape can see all of the elements in it. It does not involve the adjustment to absent or unseen factors (Köhler, 1925, pp. 53 *ff*, 276 *f*). Köhler thinks this a very important point. He indicates that tests which place before an animal a series of nonsense stimuli with most of the problem hid, are apt to be quite unreliable as tests of animal intelligence. There are a whole set of influences stimulating the ape. He is already habituated to respond to different aspects of the situation. Thus there is in operation a complex of habit tendencies or ecphorized engrams of a more or less concordant nature in connection with the present original responses. The objective constitutes a central stimulus to these responses in association with facilitation and gradient domination. The reaction pattern of the ape thus contains the background necessary to a co-ordination and integration which will give a correct solution of the problem. It is undoubtedly the effecting of an integration by the interaction of these responses which Köhler calls " insight." Such behaviour on the part of the ape is apparently as complex as, and probably even more complexly organized than, that of the subjects responding with only a short-delayed reaction. Also, the factors operative in delayed response such as residual kinæsthetic and muscular responses of a relatively plastic and temporary or mnemic nature, enabling the animal to retain absent stimuli, even for a short delay, would greatly facilitate the integration of behaviour called " insight." We must also remember that an organism is a dynamic unit with irradiation, facilitation, and more than mere additive summation of behaviour tendencies and impulses.   These give some further important cues for a more adequate and detailed explanation of this type of behaviour.

Such behaviour as we have been discussing, however, seems to be relatively short in duration and somewhat infrequent in occurrence.   Thus it is not as important in behaviour as it might otherwise be.   Apes, taken in the long run, are about as stupid as humans.

If this type of mediate response, as shown by the apes, also probably some dogs, and some children (Walton's and Hunter's experiments—this type of response for the raccoons is questionable on account of the possibility of motor or other cues), is called by the vague term "thinking," it need not be assumed that reflective thinking is present, nor can " thinking " be regarded as an explanation. However, such behaviour, particularly of the ape, does at least represent an intermediate or sub-symbolic stage between immediate response and reflective behaviour.

Concerning reflective thinking, the term implies an immediately potential self-awareness or reference and the attachment of " meaning " to acts and objects.   For this attachment of meaning, the act or object must be represented in the ape's behaviour system as a stimulus in order for reactions to occur toward it as another part of the ape's behaviour.   While the act or object is not represented in this manner, the object of meaning or of response is relatively outside, although not separate from, the ape's behaviour system.   Thus one side of the meaning equation is not adequately given in the ape's own responses. Further, for self-awareness or reference to exist, there must be a somewhat developed integration of the " self " in behaviour.   From the analysis of symbols, previously given, it will be seen that these requirements of reflective thinking are met in symbolic integration and not before. Perhaps a more specific and preferable term for reflective thinking is reflective behaviour[1] ; consequently, it will be used hereafter to designate the characteristics given above.

[1] Indicating that one part of behaviour is reacting toward another part of behaviour in the manner peculiar to symbolic differentiation.

Such characteristics of reflective behaviour do not seem to be given in the ape's activity. The process involved is apparently one of integrating relatively separate reactions into a total response. A situation in relatively loose connection with behaviour is being directly defined by the response of the ape and their integration toward the situation. It is not responses in the behaviour of the organism itself which are being defined, thus giving both parts of a meaning equation therein. This is shown by the evident lack of the ability of the ape to use symbols or adequately substitute within its behaviour a representative of an absent stimulus, a tool for example. In reality it is, as already indicated, a type of behaviour similar to, although more complex than, the dog's analysis of the fence obstacle previously discussed.

Some observers of child behaviour have assumed that a child, before it has developed language habits, " understands " the meaning of words. This is perhaps true, if by understanding it is meant that he is conditioned to respond with a certain response to a given word, just as a horse has learned to start at a clicking sound, a dog comes when called, a chick runs for food at the hen's cluck, or as any other animal may have established a conditioned response. There seems no adequate reason to assume an " understanding " in a reflective sense ; the child's behaviour may be accounted for otherwise.

Further, there has been considerable discussion as to the remarkable ability of the child, after he has acquired symbols, to generalize and use symbols appropriately for a large number of similar objects or situations. Upon a slightly critical examination, this assumption regarding the child's ability to manipulate abstract characteristics is found to be exactly the opposite. It is the child's inability to discriminate differences. The gestalt psychologists have demonstrated how different stimuli may have the same value due to certain configurations on a background. This characteristic of using a symbol for similar situations is similar to the behaviour of the adult who calls everything a tree which is tall, has rough bark and branches, or who calls anything with coloured petals a flower. This would not represent a great understanding or power of generalizing about trees or flowers in the eyes of a botanist. Nor does the fact that a child overlooks such differences show great abstract powers—rather it shows lack of experience and ignorance.

In the older children and adults there are more complex mediate responses to stimuli covering long periods of time. From this standpoint we have annihilated both time and space. The adjustment process is interrupted, delayed and stretched out.

The most complete and adequate explanation of this delay is to be found in the functioning of symbolic mechanisms whereby symbols are substituted for acts and objects. Thus the causal gap is filled in for this type of mediate response. Self-integration and " awareness " are aspects of the symbolic process, due to the fact that the symbol in its integration involves the differentiation of the " self " from " others," as has been previously described. Symbols also furnish a basis for so-called meaning.

The problem of meaning must receive more specific analysis. The basis which makes meaning possible is the sequential or functionally dependent relationship existing between parts of behaviour. Of course, before meaning has arisen in behaviour, it does not exist as such ; however, the functional relationships do definitely exist. For instance, a wriggling string stimulates the cat to chase it ; if meaning were present, a string would mean something " to be chased." Food stimulates the dog to eat ; if meaning were present, food would mean " something to eat." Similarly, as was loosely said before in regard to the dog's analysis of the fence, if meaning were present the meaning of the fence would be given in the dog's responses to it. Causally or functionally speaking, the meaning for a person of any act or object exists in the total responses to it both mnemic and original in association with other individuals and objects. For example, the meaning of the act " hello " is found in the response to it both by others and by oneself. One does not say " hello " to a post— at least under ordinary circumstances—it is a meaningless

gesture.   The meaning of turning an electric switch is to
be found in the complex responses made to the light coming
on, otherwise turning a switch becomes nonsense.   Thus
the basis for meaning exists causally in all behaviour.

Now, for the meaning of an act or object to appear as a
distinct part of behaviour, it is necessary, as explained,
for the organism to produce a stimulus which is a substitute
for the act or object, but at the same time is differentiated
by definite responses from the act or object, and responds
to this self-stimulation.   This is exactly what occurs in
symbolic activity.   Thus meaning is behaviour of a particular type.   It consists in responding to a stimulus
symbol.   One part of behaviour represents the object or
act and this first part is being defined by the other parts of
behaviour.   It is the first part of behaviour—representing
the act or object—in which analysis takes place ; thus the
analysis takes place in the object.   This analysis is carried
on by the responses toward the part of behaviour representing the object.

In order to avoid the accusation that meaning has been
surreptitiously smuggled into behaviour, the explanation
of the genesis of symbols by social behaviour and social
interchange of stimuli must be recalled.   This process of
the integration of symbols was explained in terms of the
behaviour of interacting organisms.

The behaviour system represents a remarkable mechanism of analysis and definition of complex stimuli.   Within
a symbolizing behaviour system there is one part of the
integrated behaviour which stimulates and presents absent
situations, past events, possible future events—the whole
range of the universe for which adequate symbols are at
hand.   Another part is in process of making original
responses, also auxiliary and residual mnemic responses
which are possible due to the past experience, habits, and
bodily processes which are present.   How complex this
system of reaction tendencies may be can be partially realized
when we consider the processes already described as well
as the complex behaviour observed in other animals.
The plasticity which exists in the sub-symbolic delayed-

response mechanisms shown in the dog's or ape's behaviour and even more developed in humans is operative. With such an integrated symbolizing behaviour system operating as a unit, there are the processes necessary for analysing and defining, for getting the meaning of our universe both social and physical.

This causal analysis of reflective behaviour and of meaning given above holds some important implications for knowledge. We do not know objects directly, but only indirectly through substituting some act representative of them and thus stimulating ourselves to respond to the substitutions as we would to the objects themselves. This involves a mechanism of interchangeable stimuli through which persons may take the rôle of the act or object. This means that knowledge as such rests upon a sufficiently consistent use of these stimuli by both parties. Too great an inconsistency robs them of their adequacy as substitute stimuli, and confusion, not knowledge, is present. Due to similarities between individuals, they have been able to develop a large body of consistently interchangeable stimuli.

This fact of mutual interdependence means that knowledge, meaning and ideas are not confined within a skull of the cerebral cortex—however important this centralizing mechanism is—but exist as a social process observable and analysable. Social interaction is essential just as the cerebral cortex is necessary, and as long as this is true reflective behaviour cannot be said to be confined to one exclusive of the other, as some would wish to confine it to the brain. An analogy with tennis playing may serve to illustrate the point. The play of muscles in the individuals is a very important and essential part, but the game consists in essence of the interplay between the players in which rackets, balls, net, and court are also essential. An observer confining his attention exclusively to the muscles of a player might be inclined to place the tennis game there, but this would hardly give us an adequate account of the process of the game. Nor will brain processes alone give us an adequate account of reflective behaviour. A man who is genuinely alone, socially speaking, *i.e.*, freed from all social influences, cannot " know " anything. Actually cut a man from his fellows, in " isolation," and you cut his mind in two, leaving not two dead halves, but dissolution. Thought is impossible. Knowledge must be obtained by the confirmation of potential symbols by social action and behaviour—otherwise it is meaningless. Separate man from the confirmatory reactions and response of others and his universe of knowledge tumbles. The fact that a person can for a time accept a substitute confirmation is apparently incidental. There must be recurrence for knowledge. The more exact the recurrences, the more confirmed and clear the knowledge ; also, the more general the recurrences, the more established is the known apt to be.

The indirect character of the symbol is also emphasized by the analysis of Ogden and Richards (1923) in the *Meaning of Meaning*, in which they attempt to formulate a basis for a science of symbolism. They give a very suggestive account of symbol-situations. They insist upon the distinction of the symbol from the object symbolized, going so far as to say that only an imputed relation exists between the symbol and the referent or object symbolized. However, this statement, as well as their repeated insistence upon it, might mislead the less critical reader into the conception that the connection is less close than it actually is. While the connection is partially indirect, it is not arbitrary, as their treatment might lead some to think. Even in those cases where symbols do appear to be quite arbitrary, such as in Algebra for instance, this arbitrariness depends upon a frame of reference which is so highly standardized that symbols may be shifted according to agreement with it. But the frame of reference itself rests and depends upon intricately adjusted and agreed standards of action which are anything but arbitrary. It is true that the symbol may be arbitrary in its superficial aspect before it becomes a symbol. That is, originally there may be no relation between " mama " and " mother " before " mama " begins to be associated with the mother. But when it becomes a symbol *in action* for mother, *more action* ; no amount of logical abstraction can do away with a causal relation similar to that which holds regarding the other responses of the child to the mother and the relation is something more than a merely " imputed relation."

It may be somewhat arbitrary, whether a person eats prunes or dates for breakfast ; but having eaten, all the cathartics and emetics which may be applied cannot do away with a causal relation established between the individual and the prunes or dates, although it may change the character of the causal relation in some important respects. Neither is a symbol, after it is integrated, something arbitrary. A symbol also represents direct causal relation. It is probable that these writers would not insist upon its too arbitrary character if pressed for a closer analysis on this point, particularly in view of their emphasis upon the fact that meaning is dependent upon the relation in a psychological context. Not enough consideration of the essential social factors in symbolic integration is perhaps responsible for their attribution of a greater arbitrariness to symbols than can accurately be assigned to them. Of course, their criticism of certain fetish characteristics of symbols is sound on another basis, and the distinction between a symbol and the object symbolized is necessary and valid.

Such an explanation of meaning as has been given above shows that all knowledge is acquired in the same manner. Our knowledge of so-called physical objects is not " known " in a different manner than our knowledge of good, or bad, or progress. However, there are important differences between knowing one thing and another. These are the specific causal processes involved. The only difference between " seeing " a chair in which one may sit and " seeing " one in which one cannot sit is a matter of the causal factors involved, and not a difference in the process of knowing. The latter involves causal sequences which do not involve the actual presence of the chair, and in some cases sequences which are called pathological. It is

the causal or functional analysis which is the important
task in analysing knowledge. To say that we know a physical
object in the same manner that we know an idea is not to
confuse the symbol with the object symbolized, the
symbol tree with the tree itself, for instance. It merely
means that to " know " either of these objects requires
the symbolization of them and responses toward this
symbol ; that is, the operation of the symbolic behaviour
mechanisms.

Certain important facts for introspective psychology
are to be drawn from this explanation of reflective
behaviour. In reflective behaviour there are the differentiating responses representing or symbolizing the act
or object. The completeness with which the object is
analysed depends upon both the ability to take the rôle
of the object and also the completeness with which the
other differentiating responses operate. The main fallacy
of the introspectionist is the assumption that we know
directly instead of indirectly by such symbolic behaviour.
He assumes that we can know directly by direct observation of so-called sensory and central processes. According
to the previous analysis, the method of obtaining knowledge
is seen to be indirect by the use of symbols. Hence, we
are unable to know what the central processes are until we
are able to symbolize them to some degree, not by direct
introspection. At present we are not able to symbolize
central process adequately enough to make even this
method as profitable as desirable. We may symbolize a
strained feeling in the region of the eyes just as we can
symbolize a pain in the abdomen. But we can hardly
introspect for the causal sequence behind the strain in the
head any more than we can introspect to see whether we
have appendicitis or not. In either case, we lack sufficiently fine symbolic integrations to carry on a very
extensive analysis, even when aided by instruments for
attacking the causal factors involved. The technique of the
Freudians and the psycho-analysts gives us very clear
evidence that the so-called introspective attempt at direct
observation is a failure. The subject is often unable to

directly get at mnemic connections which, if allowed to
run off under their own ecphoric influences, easily come to
light through causal connections.

Such a verbal report as given in free association and
the like is not to be confused with introspection.   In the
verbal report the stimulus-situation and symbol are being
responded to (the stimulus fallacy for introspection), and
it is the analysis contained in these responses which is
valid.   It is not an attempted description of so-called
internal process by the subject.   The verbal report is in
principle the same as a chemist's analysis of Sodium.   The
controls and conditions are, of course, much different, but
the method of reaction is the same.

As a matter of fact, what the introspectionist regards as
a unique method is either a *cul de sac* or merely the application of the method of observation used in all sciences.
There is some difference in the objects analysed, but the
method is the same.   For the usual introspection does not
analyse so-called sensory or central process as such, but
some stimulus symbol which has been imputed to the
central processes and which are not sufficiently representative of them simply because we have not yet the
knowledge to make them so.   At present we are able to
integrate few substitute acts or symbols which can be
adequately checked causally as being representative of
these internal processes.   We lack in technique.   As soon
as we have adequately formed symbols of these central
processes, introspection may amount to something, but it
will have changed faces on us—it will no longer be introspection as it is now technically considered.   It will be
a behaviouristic analysis, even though it may be practised
upon one's self.   If introspection merely meant a behaviouristic analysis of one's responses, there could hardly be
objection to it.   Nor could objection be found to such a
procedure on the ground that it is in the responses of
individuals that the analysis occurs.   All analysis is of
this nature.   But the analysis of one's own responses will
amount to a great deal more when the idea that we can
directly know them is exchanged for the conception that

their analysis is to be found in dependent and associated behaviour relationships and sequences.

Now most of our so-called introspection is merely the manipulation of symbols similar to any reasoning or thinking process. It is not a direct observation of " sensory " or central brain processes. Most of the value which so-called introspection has contributed has been on another score than that of introspection. It has been a result of the observation of human behaviour on the same basis as we observe all things of which we have knowledge— the same manner in which any stimulus is examined, either by a physicist or a chemist, or a so-called introspectionist.

This point needs special consideration. Knowledge is a result of symbolization in a behaviour framework. All knowledge apparently is obtained through the process of behaviour responses to stimuli, from the chemist to the psychologist or sociologist. The chemist has symbols for different chemicals. He may perform certain specific response to test the validity of the symbol to represent the substance. He may also control the conditions under which he makes the analysing responses whereby he knows the symbolized substance. This knowledge is held together by symbolization. The psychologist labels certain responses, " imagery " for example, but he has much less control first, in determining whether the reaction is actually made —the chemist has little difficulty in testing a white granulated substance for salt—and second, in discovering the causal relations of the reaction if it is present. The method of knowing is the same, however, in either case. The stringency of control and check on the causal sequence is the essential difference in method between a so-called very accurate piece of knowledge, such as the law of gravity, for instance, and the most flighty piece of knowledge, such as a day-dream fantasy. A large number of persons who argue for introspection are not really arguing for introspection, but merely for what they confuse with introspection, namely, the application of our only means of obtaining knowledge to behaviour and social facts. The study of what a stimulus-symbol is, be it the symbol

" image " or a stone, is not introspection as such. It is probably necessary to recall that while the symbol stone and a particular stone are different, the known or knowledge aspects are similar in either case, and this is the point being emphasized. The symbol stone has as content the behaviour responses to stone themselves, as well as to the actions of persons pertaining to stones, which responses have subsequently been directed toward the symbol, thus giving it content ; also a particular stone is not known as such without the attachment of this symbolic character which the stone-stimulus takes on. Thus a particular stone is in reality a symbol, and hence calls forth these same responses to it.[1] In the above discussion it is this common method of making responses of knowing which is similar in both cases, so that the distinction between the symbol and the object symbolized is not being ignored or confused. The distinction may be taken care of by the statement that the causal connections are different in the different situations. The emphasis here is upon the method of knowing which is the similarity being pointed out without neglecting the fact that symbols have specific content processes which differ. It is usually when an individual tries to look directly inside at his own brain action or, as usually put, directly in at his own so-called sensory processes or sense data, without adequate instruments to see what he is trying to look for, that he may be properly said to have " introspected."

Further in regard to the verbal report, as such it is useful. Such a report, however, must be considered causally as a response to stimuli and not so much as a report symbolically valid on its face. As a matter of fact, the scientific study of all speech reactions requires the application of a similar methodological principle ; namely, speech reactions are primarily to be considered causally or functionally as a response to the total stimulus situation before the reagent. Thus, for instance, responses to a questionnaire give us

---

[1] A study of optical responses and so-called optical illusions will convince one that we see what we " know how " to see ; by no means can we abstract ourselves from our past.

information concerning speech reactions to it, and are not
to be considered as merely responses to an hypothetical
situation proposed in a question.   Only after analyses of
the stimulus can it be judged whether the response is
mainly to the hypothetical situation or to the other
aspects involved, and then it remains to be seen whether
the response is similar when the hypothetical situation is
actually encountered.   For example, a question, " Have you
a prejudice against negroes ? " may be answered in the
negative, while in reality the person would strenuously
object to fraternal relations with coloured people.   Application of the above methodological principle should put
us on guard against such speech reactions—all are to be
regarded as responses to the whole stimulus-situation,
which naturally may be so well defined in some cases that
a verbal response can be causally well defined.

Now regarding the analysis of the symbolic process,
this has been attempted here on the same basis as that on
which all scientific analysis of knowledge is carried on.   It
has been studied, not as a process of introspection, but as
an objective social process observable and subject to
analysis with the symbolic tools and behaviour response
available.   It is becoming more and more possible to put
this process into a frame of measurement where different
observers can obtain the same result.   The antithesis
between subjective and objective drops out of the way.
The mysterious thing called imagination turns out to be a
constructive phase of the symbolic process capable of
statement in scientific terms.   Imagination may designate
a play with symbols, or in a more active sense, an integration and redintegration of social objects, future plans,
social situations, and the like.   While the symbolic process
may be somewhat difficult to observe in all respects until
we have developed more precise symbolic behaviour
patterns with which to observe it, yet it may be studied as
a causal process, using as checks the more tested parts of
knowledge, while indicating certain aspects requiring more
substantial corroboration.   The symbolic process of
acquiring knowledge can be turned upon the symbolic

process itself, just as it can be turned upon chemistry and physics or mathematics. The fact that with particular people at particular times the symbolic process may not be observable does not thus show the process itself to be out of range of observation. The important fact is that it is observed upon innumerable occasions and as a process, the period of integration in children being particularly instructive. We " see " or symbolize it in essentially the same manner that the biologist, for example, " sees " the operation of cells and the mechanisms of heredity, or the economist sees a business cycle. In either case more perfected technique is, of course, desirable.

It is clear that such an analysis places the symbolic process as observable and objective, or more preferable, non-subjective, as compared with the usual use of subjective. To say it is observable does not mean that its colour must be named. It might also be difficult to name the colour of a tennis game or a dog fight, yet both are quite observable. If observing Pavlov's reflex is objective, in the same way observing the symbolic process, ideas, etc., is also objective. Both are performed by similar behaviour processes. We observe with all of our responses and not only with seeing, hearing, and the like. To assume that so-called sense data and sensory processes are the elementary form of knowledge is not warranted. It is the social interchange in symbolic integration which gives us knowledge.

There are two senses in which the symbolic process may be called subjective : first, in an anthropocentric, or personal, sense—the reference of acts and objects to one's self as a subject ; second, it is a region of the constructions of new objects and may thus be called subjective in the sense that the new symbol is in process, but not yet integrated. If someone wishes arbitrarily to use the term " subjective " to apply to anything going on inside a person, the use by strict definition might be legitimate, but it should apply to heart or gland action as adequately as to brain action, and would only be partially and in a limited sense descriptive of the symbolic process. Or if one wishes arbitrarily to designate those symbols in which the causal factors seem to be predominantly personal, that may be legitimate if the use of it is thus understood. Subjective, however, needs considerable sterilization before it can be used thus with assurance of proper connotation. But an application of the term "subjective" to the symbolic process, or to ideas as a label of unobservability, and as antithetical to objective is not sufficiently accurate ; also the general use of the term itself is too loose to be of practical use in this respect. To designate the two aspects already indicated seems to be the most accurate use of the term "subjective," and then it is used at the risk of considerable. misunderstanding. To show the observable and objective character of reflective behaviour does not necessarily mean an attack upon an individual's personal existence or activity which he feels particularly his own, but it should help to disclose more clearly the character and nature of such existence. Further, the symbolic process is only one of the many phases of the behaviour of individuals.

Neither the symbolic process nor reflective behaviour are to be identified with so-called images. " Images," as immediate responses, apparently may exist without symbols. But for " images " to become objects of reflective behaviour the symbolic process must be present, although not necessarily in spoken symbols. Head's (1920–21) experiments, upon aphasia patients suffering from unilateral lesions, indicate that apparently images may function at least in the absence of the proper use of spoken words. Certain patients, being absent from their room, could not accurately describe in words the location of the furniture, but could do so by pointing.

Neither is reflective behaviour to be confined to the operation of the vocal and subvocal[1] apparatus, although its genesis evidently lies here. Any act or object capable of symbolic reference may involve reflective behaviour.

It seems apparent from the analysis of the symbolic process that knowledge, as this term is generally used, exists only through this process of symbolization.

Max Müller, who was an ardent exponent of the proposi-

---

[1] *Vide* an interesting experiment by Agnes Thorson (1925) in regard to tongue movements and thinking.

tion that we cannot think without the use of words, gives
the following illustration of an attempt to do so.   The
illustration may not prove anything, and certainly it
does not prove that thoughts and words, in the narrow
sense, are the same, even though words are necessary in
order that thought function.   Of course, if within the
meaning of the term " word " there are included all the
responses going with it which make it a symbol, we have
a much better case, for thinking certainly consists of
the process of symbolization.

The experiment is an interesting one, to say the
least.

. . . " I now proceed to describe a counter-experiment,
or rather the fruitless efforts which some philosophers have
made in order to prove that they could conceive a simple
concept, at least, such as dog, without having a name for
it.   I have described the same experiment before, and if
it seemed childish, all I can say is that this is not my fault.
We are told that people have to begin by shutting their
eyes and ears, and holding their breath.   They then sink
into some kind of semi-consciousness, and when all is dark
and still, they try their new art of ventriloquism, thinking
thought without words.   They begin with a very simple
case.   They want to conjure up the thought of a—I must
not say what, for it is to be a nameless thing, and every
time that its name rises it is gulped down and ordered
away.   However, in confidence, I may whisper that they
want to conjure up the thought of a dog.

" Now the word dog is determinately suppressed ;
hound, cur, and all the rest, too, are strictly excluded.
Then begins the work.   ' Rise up, thou quadruped with
ears and a wagging tail ! '   But alas ! the charm is broken
already.   Quadruped, ears, tail, wagging, all are words
which cannot be admitted.

" Silence is restored, and a new effort begins.   This
time there is to be nothing about quadruped, or animal,
or hairy brute.   The inner consciousness sinks lower, and
at last there rises a being to be developed gradually and
insensibly into a dog.   But alas ! ' being ' too is a word,

L

and as soon as it is whispered, all the nameless dogs vanish into nothing.

" A last appeal, however, remains. No animal, no being is to be talked of ; complete silence is restored ; no breath is drawn. There is something coming near, the ghost appears, when suddenly he is greeted by the recogniz-ing self with Bow-wow, bow-wow ! Then, at last, the effort is given up as hopeless, the eyes are opened, the ears unstopped, the breath is allowed to rise again, and as soon as the word dog is uttered, the ghost appears, the concept is there, we know what we mean, we think and say Dog. Let anyone try to think without words, and, if he is honest, he will confess that the process which he has gone through is somewhat like the one I have just tried to describe " (1887, p. 58–59).

The fundamental character of the integration of the self has been referred to in numerous places. Special considera-tion of this social fact should be included in connection with the subject of reflective behaviour.

When the child first develops " self " and symbolic integration, the " self " plays an outstanding rôle, as we have pointed out in various places. It is not so much due to the fact that the child is ego-centric or " believes " himself to be the centre of the universe as that he actually is the centre of his " known " universe. His own behaviour becomes a centre of symbolization and know-ledge for him.

The self-centred character of the child's thinking has been analysed very strikingly by Piaget (1926), whose researches show that it is not until about seven or eight years that the child is able to take the point of view of the other person. He calls this period up to seven years the period of ego-centric thought. Following it begins the period of socialized thought. The use of " socialized " in this sense is unfortunate on account of the implication that the integration preceding is not social. This is decidedly not true. The facts previously stressed should be sufficient to show its pre-eminent social character. However, a greater degree of social integration becomes possible when, according to Piaget, at about seven to eight the child learns to reflectively place himself in the rôle of the other person, a thing which, it is evident from our analysis, he has before been doing unreflectively.

The symbolic beginnings in a child must necessarily be centred around himself as a basis. His symbols are dependent upon his social experience, which are naturally limited to experiences relating quite directly to his own behaviour in association with others. During this early period when integration centres around the self, symbols are accepted dogmatically; they are fixed words and are true for everybody. The child naïvely assumes this universal validity. Consequently, there is no basis in experience for reflectively placing himself in the viewpoint of other persons in making explanations to other children or adults. However, Piaget's assumption (1926, p. 41) that there is no real interchange of thought here is somewhat gratuitous in certain respects. Where there is common experience, children do obviously understand each other, and much more so do they understand adults as Piaget states. Where there is insufficient common experience, interchange of thought, even between sophisticated adults, is handicapped until this experience is acquired. The only basis for saying that there is no interchange is that the child's thinking is drawn from a common social process, but there is certainly interchange in this process. However, in justice to Piaget, apparently his main point is that previous to 7–8 there is an absence in the child of this reflective taking of the other's point of view in communication, and here he is evidently on sound ground, assuming, as appears probable, that his observations are typical in this respect. It is unfortunate that Piaget does not check his observations, which were obtained under the conditions of the institute, by more extensive observations upon children under more normal conditions, or at least by more definitely making allowances for such differences. His conclusions must be qualified on this score, and obviously some of them will have to be modified in consideration of other data, particularly those data pertaining to the social factors in the child's reflective behaviour. The observations in the institute do not seem to give a wholly rounded picture of the child's symbolic activity, or perhaps some of its important aspects were more easily overlooked.

Piaget's encumbrance with the psycho-analysts' conception of a subconscious source of a self-generated autistic type of thought lies back of his conception of its non-social character, and permits him to ignore its essential social aspects. Such a conception can hardly stand scientific analysis. There is undoubtedly a great deal going on, such as stress and strain, vague feelings, etc., in any live organism, man or other animal, which it cannot symbolize and hence cannot think reflectively about, but there seems no adequate reason for labelling this as subconscious thought, even though these processes may exert a great amount of influence upon the reflective behaviour. Further, after a child has learned to think, the early symbols and experiences may be apparently buried in a mass of later symbolic acquirement. The early experiences of a child, particularly when the symbolic world is so fixed and universal as is early childhood, may furnish very apt material for sympathies, antipathies, and complexes. These may be later submerged, but are not independently developed. The point which must be emphasized in this connection is that this " thought " is socially derived and integrated, and not autistically developed in the sense of independent self-generation. The Freudians and the psychoanalysts have certainly given us important facts regarding these buried and non-rational complexes, but there is no need of complicating the affair by unnecessary and unfounded assumptions which cannot account for their origin except in some mysterious conception. To speak then of this early period as one of non-communicable thought (Piaget, 1926, p. 45), if by " thought " he meant so-called reflective or ideational thinking, is a contradiction of the facts and of the conception which identifies such thought with symbolic operation, which Piaget apparently accepts in general.   It must be remembered that *all* living organisms have a great amount of non-symbolic impulses, visceral activity, glandular secretion, habits and experience which exert powerful influences and which the organism is not yet able to symbolize—reflective behaviour is still young !   Our task is to turn our research technique upon these phenomena rather than to ban them to the realm of non-communicable thoughts.

With the expanding social experiences of the child, he comes into contact with larger numbers of symbols and with more persons and groups.   From such experience he learns that there are unexpected and contradictory reactions to the same symbol.   He learns that a " word has several names," that his parents do not " know everything." Communication begins to be something more than saying certain words—it becomes a matter of saying the words which will elicit an understanding response from the other.   Piaget's splendid work contains illustrations and materials indicating this development. At 7—8, he indicates, there is the beginning of the causal— in a more strict sense—stage of thought, in contrast to the period up to seven years[1] in which mechanical or logical causality is not a subject of consideration on the part of the child.   The causal stage of thought has its source and development, as Piaget indicates (1926, Ch. V), in the human or anthropocentric experiences and motivations.

Thus we see that underlying reflective behaviour is the stress and strain and the dynamics of the organism as it

---

[1] Koffka says that " causality soon comes to play an important rôle " (1924, p. 331), and cites three examples showing the conception of cause at the ages four years, four years, and four years and ten months for three children.   One child said to his mother, who was sewing, " But you can't see anything, for I have my eyes closed," clearly indicating an idea of causality.   However, the idea of cause expressed above is quite animistic rather than mechanical, and Piaget does well to differentiate here.   It will be valuable to have this sort of observation extended to include more cases.

interacts with other organisms. Symbolic behaviour in the child develops as a social integration and first centres largely around the child's own social experiences. With the growth of the child's social contacts, he is able at about 7–8 (this age can be tentatively accepted) to reflectively put himself in another's place. It is not until about 11–12, according to Piaget (1926, p. 196), that the child begins to hold hypotheses as such, to draw conclusions from them, and to see whether these conclusions are justified or not.

At the beginning of symbolic development, everything is personal and endowed with personal qualities. With greater expansion of personal and group experience, more intermediate and causal experiences are analysed and symbolized. Objects become differentiated into non-personal, physical and personal objects—but still by the use of social stimuli. Physical objects are known by reacting to them as others react toward the objects and by reacting to others in connection with their own reaction to the physical objects. Thus they become known to us by the same method that is used to know social objects. In this sense all physical objects are indirectly social objects. In the scientist, reflective behaviour has gone to the degree that the immediate personal elements of symbolization may be out of sight. It is in this respect that symbolic development has reached a most complicated form. The symbolic aspect of the personality of the abstract thinker has become so finely integrated that it may become an interplay of symbols without the ego holding down one side, as is usually the case in less abstract reflective behaviour, and often the case even with the scientist. The person (or ego) may merely manipulate the symbols in order to derive a balanced result. Symbolic development apparently is by means of an expanding content and experience which comes to include as much of the universe as possible within its compass. In such an expansion the person's personal reactions become merely one among many other similar ones, and not the centre of creation. However, few people are able to thus treat themselves statistically or quantitatively, even to meet the requirements of this effective type of symbolic integration.

To be able to carry on such complex reflective behaviour does not mean, however, that personal considerations and sympathies are ignored in social life. Working in and giving substance to the symbolic process is the whole of individual and social experience. The more complex the symbolic integration, the more effective it may be as a means of facilitating social experience, realizing personal and social ideals, and serving to develop the æsthetic phases of life. Also, such emotional factors seem to be of considerable importance in motivating and resolving reflective behaviour and in fixing engramic experiences which serve as content to symbolic behaviour. Excitation involving strong emotion results in greater mnemic impressions, as Semon states, and which is a well-attested fact of behaviour.

However, the use of symbols as emotional and æsthetic stimuli and as a means of establishing facts and analysing causal factors should be differentiated. These are two different, although not separate, phases of the symbolic process. Special techniques, such as art and literature, are developed for the manipulation of emotional and æsthetic experience. Certain symbols function very often as stimuli for strong emotional arousal. Symbols may not lose their symbolic character by such use as Ogden and Richards (1923, pp. 261–71) at times seem somewhat ready to assume, they might even become more potent as symbols by more complete ecphory of engrams, or they may become different symbols. Of course, at some times symbols do undoubtedly lose their character as symbols and merely stimulate as rhythmic sounds and the like, but usually there remains some symbolic content. The symbol must not be thought of as a too static integration.

On the other hand, we have special techniques for eliminating too personal emotions in symbolic behaviour. The scientific technique has been most successful in this respect. But even here an emotional drive for obtaining tested knowledge seems an essential aspect.

The basic nature of self-integration as a part of the symbolic process is also illustrated by the phenomena of dual personality. Separate symbolic integrations appear so closely associated with each one of these distinct selves that in some cases there is little obvious transfer of experience from one to the other. The person is said to be " unconscious " or has no memory of what the other self, which is not immediately in control, has done. The normal personality has centres of symbolic integration around its different selves in a similar manner, but ordinarily they are all more or less effectively interconnected into a central or composite self for which symbols have a general validity. The dual personality is merely an extreme case.

It is perhaps well to indicate in this connection that by so-called consciousness is generally meant a symbolic self-integration. When symbols become habitual or automatic it is probable that the self-reference has greatly diminished or is near the minimum. Such enticing problems as these are ones for special and more extended social research.

Another interesting question is, are there other means of " knowing " similar to reflective behaviour which go beyond symbols requiring a more complex behaviour integration? The conviction on the part of various trained and serious scientists that telepathy occurs as well as the large amount of serious attention given to such subjects as clairvoyance and the like are sufficient to warn one against being dogmatic on the possibility of other forms of thinking and knowing. All such discussions as that of Ouspensky (1922), for example, in regard to the possibility of fourth-dimensional thought or intuition cannot be nonchalantly dismissed by a serious thinker in spite of some quite evident fallacies. The scientific determination and analysis of intuitive or immediated knowing, should it exist, would obviously be very significant. There is the definite possibility that other forms of thought occur, or, if there is not yet a more complex type of knowing, that such may in the future be integrated in behaviour processes. It is one of the first tasks of the scientist to be open-minded to any of these possibilities ; however, with our present knowledge, these questions are generally placed in the hypothetical or philosophical realm.

We are sure there is a large part of behaviour experience perhaps carried to a considerable degree in the emotional content of symbols which influences reflective behaviour in a remarkable subtle manner, and frequently involves contradictory or non-rational behaviour. Psychologists have clearly disclosed the irrational man, activated by influences of which he may be unaware. This is perhaps another way of saying that our symbols and reflective behaviour are products of our total experience. It is a place for more sociological investigation to supplement the data of the psychologist.

If the engramic theory holds true regarding the engramic effects of stimuli upon the germ cells, and there are some facts which point in this direction, it may be that the mechanisms underlying symbolic integration will be to a greater and greater degree transmitted by heredity, giving the infant during its plastic period a cumulative advantage of centuries of transmission of these engramic effects. Of course, the inheritance of a modicum of acquired traces is yet an open question. Still, it would be possible just by the process of mutation and selection for a cumulation of hereditary mechanisms which facilitate symbolic integration. Further, expansion in symbolic development should give greater possibilities of a new type of integration. For instance, a considerable amount of enlargement of symbolic content is undoubtedly to be obtained by studying processes in their backward sequence as well as in their forward sequence, which is our usual method of analysis. Jesperson, in applying the backward method to the study of the origin of language, has undoubtedly contributed a greater accuracy to his knowledge of it. History still remains to be written backwards. No one knows how much it will disclose which has previously been mysterious. Karl Pearson suggests that, if one could travel away from the earth more rapidly than light travels,

he would see events backwards.   A man would begin life
at death and end it at birth.   A study of processes from all
possible angles is advantageous in contributing to symbolic
facility.   Further, if scientific advance begins to put
greater and greater amount of dynamics and movement
into our knowledge content, we will require a greater and
greater symbolic facility to keep knowledge within our
grasp.   If behaviourism has placed emphasis upon the
dynamic side of behaviour phenomena, the Gestalt theorists have compounded it.   As a matter of fact, most people
have trouble " seeing " or symbolizing the world as it is
in process, and about the best that the rest can do is to see
only short sections at once.   A significant need, scientific-
ally, is the elaboration of symbols which enable us to more
adequately understand and keep our bearings in a moving
universe.

A further aspect of perhaps more present practical
significance is that pertaining to a greater understanding
of the relation of emotional fixation of engrams and particularly symbolic mechanisms.   This is of great importance, especially in the early development of the plastic
childhood period, when symbolic habits are first being
formed and mnemic traces first being established. Another
line of investigation is that regarding the idetic or vivid
imagery types ; such types undoubtedly facilitate symbolic
development.   It is important to learn the factors underlying and promoting their integration.

CHAPTER XI

SYMBOLIC ORIGINS AND THE GROUP—THE CONTENT OF
THE SYMBOLIC PROCESS

HAVING considered symbolic integration and reflective behaviour from the standpoint of interacting behaviour systems, it now remains to redirect attention to the group as such.

To the *bow-wow*, the *pooh-pooh*, the *ding-dong*, and the *yo-he-ho* theories of the origin of language may be added, with due respect to Jespersen and others, the *sing-song* theory. Although the rôle of song and rhythm may have been more or less important, a more certain aspect apparently is that regarding the origin of language in emotional situations, and probably those social situations involving sex behaviour, as Jespersen also suggests (1923, p. 433 *f*).

Symbols must have developed only after long association had conditioned instinctive cries or sounds to specific behaviour in which two or more individuals were involved. In order that the mnemic traces become sufficiently vivid and consistent to result in the necessary integration, a highly emotional state was most probably necessary. While the festive group occasion of song and dance may have served as a background, it is probable that definite sex behaviour furnished the relatively similar, recurrent, and specific activity necessary for the conditioning process associated with a highly emotional facilitating state. Specific sounds, being associated with this type of behaviour, would furnish a similar stimulus which could be produced and interchanged by each person.

Writers on language have pointed out the tendency for speech reactions to develop in adolescents, the young lovers, the newly-weds or those going through such

emotional changes.   This is also a common observation
on the part of numerous persons.   A case or two will
illustrate.   Chamberlain (1906, pp. 139 *f*) cites the case
of a young woman in late adolescence who developed a
language apparently thoroughly informed with the
necessary machinery of human speech and yet entirely
her own creation.   Two persons of my acquaintance tell
me that they developed, at the ages 42 and 60, a set of
sound symbols, about 20 in number, the meaning of which
is conveyed by the tone and context in which they are
uttered.   The attempt is to express by tonal sounds.
These two persons had developed a great regard for each
other, and it is evident that this language developed as
play and emotional expression.   They were unable to tell
me the exact meaning of the words.   Some examples
are :
>   Sūni—has different meanings on different occasions.
>   Used during a story as indicating a secret cave,
>   etc.
>   Mădis—Tone of voice indicated meaning.

The " baby-talk " of adolescents is another illustration.
It is probable that any more pronounced emotional state
tends to facilitate language behaviour—for instance,
poetical utterances by artists, or profane utterances under
emotional stress.

Apropos to the origin of language, a considerable amount
of paper has been used on discussions regarding the child's
invention of speech.   If the social origin of language is
sound, the nucleus drops out of such a discussion.   The
child comes into the world a behaviour mechanism which
is soon able to vocalize.   Symbols develop in this behaviour
process only in collaboration with other persons.   These
symbols indicate specific behaviour and any sound which
becomes properly integrated and conditioned to the parties
involved becomes a symbol.   Thus the symbol may be
unique, due to its basis in particular behaviour, however,
not as an *individual*, but as a *social* product.   If the child's
vocalizations are allowed to become thus conditioned and

integrated, there will undoubtedly arise perhaps a considerable number of unique symbols in connection with different social situations and specific experience. Various cases have been reported of children continually associated together who have developed a set of often unintelligible words whereby they have communicated with each other. The first language of the child is a special language which is understood by those concerned on the basis of specific behaviour and sounds. Upon this is integrated the native language. Vocally, the child at first has the possibility of a number of different phonetic systems. But when the native language is finally acquired, the child is then restricted according to the predominant phonetic system of that language (Vendryes, 1925). Of course, after the child has acquired symbols, he can invent other symbols for which there is a basis in action, just as a Newton can discover a scientific law, but underlying these is the pre-existing social basis.

It is after the early period that we have the age of learning secret and invented languages, beginning in some few cases as early as the sixth year. Chrisman, Hale, and others have investigated some of these phenomena. It seems that most of the argument on the invention of symbols has been beside the point. The child may furnish a new sound just as it evidently furnished " ma-ma," " pa-pa," etc., but the symbol itself is a social invention.

Although the origin of language in the race according to the previous analysis must have been the social-vocal situation, it is quite evident that the symbols were soon extended to other social gestures and signs which undoubtedly existed long previous to symbols, just as they exist now in other animal groupings. Thus there was a whole set of sign situations,[1] i.e., stimuli which functioned as signs ready to become symbol situations as soon as symbolic integration occurred.[2] In general, gesture and sign-situations form a basis for symbols. Symbols grew out of group behaviour and experience and were extended

---

[1] Sign is not being used here in a symbolic sense.

[2] See the Smithsonian Annual Report of the Bureau of Ethnology (1879–80) for a mine of information on sign language.

to include all the phases of group life.   There is no break
in the group process, only a continuation from the previous
modes of action.

Certain aspects of the symbolic content of this group
process are to be sketched in the remaining part of the
chapter.

In previous chapters the personal, personality, " self "
and " other," *i.e.*, the " human " aspects associated with
the development of symbols were elaborated.   A great
deal more could be said regarding these and other aspects
closely associated with these " personal " phases.   As an
example, Park and Burgess in a very stimulating manner
have attempted to distinguish the " meaning " and " communication " aspects from the non-symbolic aspects in
four types of social interaction ; namely, competition,
conflict, accommodation, and assimilation (1924, Ch.
VIII–XI).   Although it seems very questionable to me
(1925) whether social contact is most satisfactorily limited
to the " communicative " and " meaning " or symbolic
process phase, still this does not invalidate some important
distinctions which they have pointed out regarding the
nature of the interaction involved.   It may be admitted
—without overlooking the advantages of a wider use of
the term—that " social " may be used in a restricted sense
if the definition is clearly understood and kept in mind,
hence does not lead to confusion.   Another important
example is given in the " social attitude " and " social
value " system of sociology, as outlined, for instance, by
Thomas and Znaniecki (1920).   Such a system of sociology
rests directly for its basis upon the symbolic process.   The
stimulus-symbol represents the social value, and the
defining responses the social attitude.   Thus the social
value and the social attitude are merely opposite ends of
the same thing, and their relation is made clearer when
thought of as these phases of symbolic integration.   The
term " value " is perhaps unfortunate, but the term
" attitude " has evidently come to stay in generalizing
certain content of the social process.

However, the present purpose is to examine the content

of the symbolic process from the standpoint of the complex social act, or from the group viewpoint. The problem may be introduced and pictured briefly.

With such a knowledge of past, present, and future as the symbolic process has given, some persons have been inclined to regard symbols as having fetish powers. It seemed enough to get persons to use proper symbols for the group to maintain the activity necessary for its best interests. This is at present the naïve assumption behind a great amount of preaching as well as ethical and academic teaching. It is the old complaint, pupils are trained to give " proper " speech reactions to an instructor, but this may not mean the proper responses to the actual situation outside the classroom. The young boy still eats green apples and obese adult his chocolates in spite of admonition.

The failure of the causal experiential content of symbols to be adequate for the production of " proper conduct " in the group has resulted in the group introducing extraneous and some very drastic causal factors such as supernatural sanctions, ostracism, punishment, and the like, to give substantial body to the symbols of group behaviour. As a concrete example, there is some dispute as to whether children must have " corporal punishment " or whether they may be controlled otherwise by more indirect social means. Faris is carrying on some interesting experimentation in this latter connection. It is to be hoped that his results will soon be available and that other research will be added in this field of social control.

In view of such facts as the above it seems necessary to examine more closely what the content of the symbolic process is before going on to the problem of social control by symbols.

The facts brought out in the past chapters should have made it quite clear that symbols are developed in action and are stimuli for action. The converse of this is that symbols mean no more nor carry no more content than the social experience of the individuals of the group can bring into them. This may seem a hard statement, and certainly, in the eyes of some, will detract from the glamour of symbols, ideas, and knowledge. It means that, after all, the control of the individual and the group rests upon action and experience in the final analysis. Apparently, about the best we can do is to make the accumulation of experience less and less expensive. A main problem is how to short-cut and eliminate futile experimentation. The mobility of experience is very significant in this respect. The increased mobility made possible by symbolic behaviour (thinking and reasoning), and the utilization of experience in symbolic situations may make a small amount of experience function in many different ways, still new additional experience becomes necessary with new and changing conditions. Laboratory methods are very valuable in getting knowledge under controlled conditions, and certainly in the future we shall have to prepare and allow for much more social experimentation than we have done in the past. From the standpoint of the content of the symbolic process the question turns directly to those phases of group life which are most active and most decisive in action as being of outstanding and controlling significance in symbolic behaviour.

The field of greatest amount of group activity is that concerning the maintenance, *i.e.*, materialistic and economic, phases of social life. The overwhelming proportion of activity given to such primary interests as group maintenance is quite evident. This is true at present, and evidently was as much or more true for pre-literate peoples.

Malinowski (1923) has pointed out how symbols among preliterate people function mainly in facilitating the useful practices and arts of these people. Symbols naturally have the most favourable possibility of gaining content and precision in such behaviour.

Not only is there a very rich action basis in this phase of social life, but the action is decisive. Symbols which correlate economic activity gain clear-cut meaning. It is a matter of the life and survival or non-survival of the group and its members. The causal results are much more evident than for some other types of action.

Not only do these symbols furnish a content concerned directly with maintenance, but they furnish the body of experience upon which other and more removed symbols must depend in the main for their content, as experience and action are the only source of symbolic content. Hence, philosophies, theologies, and the like appear as outgrowths of the experiences gained in the more primary and persistent activity of the group.

The basic importance of the materialistic and economic phases of social life have been so well established that it requires little elaboration. Philosophers, historians, anthropologists, geographers, especially anthropogeographers, economists, conspicuously Marx and the historical materialists, sociologists, notably Sumner, Ward and many others have presented a large array of facts upon this subject. Such a conception of the deterministic character of material and economic factors is most consistent with the mechanistic explanation, in the sense in which it is being used as implying causal relationships with a chemical and physical basis, of the symbolic process.

Beginning with the primary dependence of the group upon these life-preserving activities, the content of the symbolic process may for convenience be divided on the one hand into those activities directly concerned with consummatory processes, preservation and sustenance, and extending to all forms of pleasurable or æsthetic enjoyment in which symbolic behaviour is involved. On the other hand, there is the symbolic content involved in the techniques, methods, principles and machinery for the production and distribution of the things necessary for sustenance, and secondarily for the enjoyment and welfare of the group. It is in this realm that knowledge and symbols find their greatest use as " means " to the " end " of group preservation and gratification. A significant part of such techniques is that called " social control." The means of control are not so essentially important in themselves, but are important as means of maintaining and ordering social behaviour to facilitate the maintenance and welfare of the group exercising the control.

M

Park and Burgess (1924, pp. 51–54) give a classification which is applicable as indicating main phases of symbolic content. It is, the economic process concerned with production and exchange of goods and particularly of values and the like, the political process including the more active questions of control, the cultural process including the shaping and defining of social forms, patterns, mores, etc., and the historical process which results in cultural continuity. By these processes the interests and welfare of the group and its members are more or less satisfactorily maintained.

A detailed elaboration of human culture would be necessary in order to completely describe the content of the symbolic process. Only the control mechanism will receive further consideration in the concluding chapter.

CHAPTER XII

THE SYMBOLIC PROCESS AND SOCIAL CONTROL

A BRIEF summary will bring together some important facts to be considered in the problem of the relation of the symbolic process and reflective control.

The trend from the individualistic subjective and structural conception to the social behaviouristic conception of the symbolic process was traced.

Symbols are integrated in a social behaviour process and their content is action. Even the so-called abstract words have this same basis. There is a continuity between man and the other animals regarding this process. Symbolic integration shows a continuity with other forms of behaviour. Symbolic behaviour is dependent upon preceding processes and represents a dynamic and continually changing phase of social life which results in new working wholes or functional unitary configurations. Causal relations are demonstrable and the presuppositions of a physical and chemical basis are valid. Thus the symbolic process is to be explained mechanistically. It is an observable process and subject to check by objective quantitative methods. Scientific laws and prediction are possible and demonstrable in this process, yet there result discoveries, inventions, creations, and new configurations unpredicted before they occur.

In regard to the origin of symbols and reflective behaviour, the integration of the social " self " and the " other " phases of personality and social life are apparently fundamental. The data examined points to definite laws and relationships holding between the development of " persons " and " personalities " and symbolic development. It is in the symbolic process that the " self " and " other " aspects arise, and *vice versa*. In the early years of childhood, symbolic behaviour centres around the self, for experience is centred here for the child. The expanding personal and group experience stimulates the development of reflective behaviour into more finely and complexly organized modes of symbolization and symbolic analysis, and also toward greater expansion of the centre of reflective behaviour to larger groupings and universes of knowledge and discourse.

The " self " and " other " aspects are group unities and exist only in social interaction, not in individuals subtracted from social interaction. The group unity is a fact and not a " fallacy." The origin and rise of symbolic behaviour requires the substitution and interchange of social stimuli. This is seen to occur in the social-vocal-auditory situation. Hence knowledge, meaning, and ideas are acquired indirectly in a social medium. A fallacy which runs through the work of a great many psychologists is the assumption that we know directly instead of indirectly by taking the rôle of the stimulus object, as shown by a social-behaviour analysis. This is the major fallacy of introspectionism.

Due to the fact that symbols in the final analysis are action words and acquired in action, they necessarily arise and function most effectively in the primary and active phases of social life, such as the basic, the maintenance, economic, and materialistic processes.

The relation of the symbolic process to social control will be discussed from two standpoints : first, the control of individual behaviour ; and second, group control. Space will permit, however, only a sketchy statement. It is a problem for much more special investigation.

In the beginning of the symbolic development of the child—and evidently of the race as well—all symbols, as previously indicated, are personal symbols on account of their genesis through interchange of personal stimuli. It is only after some development in symbolic integration that physical objects are differentiated from personal objects.

In view of the fact that the individual's self or personality is realized in symbolic integration and that this integration is a part with other personalities as well as a phase of group unity, there exists herein a very powerful means of control. The group may control individual behaviour by the manipulation of personal symbols especially. The symbolic integration of the self may be controlled by determining the kind of personality which is permissible or prized or excluded in the group. The young boy fears being called a " sissy." The derogatory term " black-leg " or " scab " exerts a powerful influence over workers. So drastic is such a term that it has been made a legal offence in some places to apply the term to a worker. The " pacifist " is pictured as a thin-blooded, weak-kneed, pale, sallow, and disreputable person. Many dangerous and ridiculous things have been done to be a " good sport." Symbols of " respectability " and " decency " must be observed. Where men or women wear only a string around the waist their dress is decent, but it is indecent to leave off the string (Sumner, 1906, p. 425). " Mohammedan women, if surprised when bathing, cover first the face " (*ibid.*, p. 421) could be said some years ago, while recently there have been public burnings of the veil.

The fact that the child's personality is only realized in the group means that this type of control may be very decisive if manipulated properly. A person is dependent, if not upon one, then another group, and ordinarily upon a whole complex of groupings for his very existence as a person. The group adds to, takes away, moulds and makes the personalities of its members. The " bad " or " good " boy is a creation of the group. Durkheim (1912) has found in studying the phenomena of suicide that in general the causes are either isolation or too great regimentation of the person in social contact. In either of these cases the personality suffers. In isolation it atrophies, in too great regimentation its distinguishing marks are done away with, and the person is lost, one among many similar ones. The control of persons is illustrated by the great amount of attention given to group opinion, to the way its members will symbolize and act toward one, to the " looking glass I " so aptly phrased by Cooley, and to the adoration for the gifts from the " dead hand " of the past.   Burgess has summarized some aspects of this type of control (1923).

The repetition of symbols may have a remarkable cumulative effect.   Semon concludes that even stimuli below the threshold of stimulation have some engramic effect, for it is well known that repeated application of a subliminal stimulus may after a time produce a regular response.

In view of the facts regarding the control of the individual by the group it is evident that persons themselves, by controlling the stimuli to which they will be subjected and the groups to which they belong, can thereby create in themselves different personalities.   The possibilities, of course, are conditioned by their past equipment and the possibility of controlling the stimuli to which they will be subjected.   Such control is sometimes quite limited, due to the influence of past experience which may be so real in present symbolic behaviour that it is hard to eliminate.   In this latter case, the concentration of activity upon the " means whereby " (Alexander, 1918) the new habits are to be established, rather than upon the old symbols and upon the end itself, may serve to integrate new and different symbols, in spite of the tendency for old habits to operate.   Activity is thus directed into a different course than the previous symbols would call for.

The behaviouristic explanation of reflective behaviour, showing how the whole body, muscles, glands and bodily organs, is involved, means that symbolic stimulation by one's self, or by others, also exerts a reciprocal influence over muscles, organs, glands, etc.   Much has been said and written about the control of the individual's organic mechanisms by such means, but as yet our knowledge is quite inadequate concerning this obviously important phase of individual organic control by symbolic behaviour. Much more specific research is needed upon this subject. Alexander (1918) represents one suggestive approach.

The control of the group is escaped often, by a life in

so-called imaginary or in substitute symbolic groups, *i.e.,* past, absent and future groups which give one a personality. This personality and personal or social status phase is a part of all reflective control, and must be adequately taken into consideration.

Within, and in addition to, these more strictly personal phases of group control, the symbols which can be integrated and configurated into the more active phases of the individual behaviour become, therefore, of greater influence in controlling the individual.

Besides the control depending upon the reflective behaviour of the individual, there are all those non-reflective modes of action which may be determined by the adequate control of the group situation including physical conditions and stimuli. Group situations are thus seen to present the social backgrounds and surroundings in which social influences, symbolic and non-symbolic, direct and limit the kind of personality which may be developed.

The next consideration, then, is the relation of the symbolic process to the group unit in which selves and personalities are determined and integrated. New and more abstract symbolic behaviour has had notable importance, as shown before, as it has been incorporated into the primary phases of social life, production, distribution, consumption, etc. It has thus been able to determine more effectively our behaviour responses. Scientific discoveries and inventions, a most important aspect of the symbolic process, have had their profoundest effects in this manner. In order that symbols may be most effective, their active configuration in group activity is necessary. Upon this primary material and economic basis, as Sumner (1906, pp. 34 *seq.*, Ch. III *passim*), following the lead of economic determinists, has well shown, are elaborated the standards or mores of maintenance. These mores consist of symbolic standards which have become common and obtained sanction as conducive to the welfare of the group in this field of collective behaviour, having grown out of group habits and folkways. Thus reflective use of physical and material

equipment, machinery, techniques, tools, methods, and
conditions of work, goods produced and living standards
is a most effective method of influencing group behaviour.
Groups and nations having similar material conditions
tend to develop similar symbolic behaviour, similar reason
and logic, and similar maintenance mores.

A further elaboration of the maintenance standards are,
according to Sumner, the secondary mores still further
removed, but resting upon the maintenance mores and
finally upon the material and economic aspects of the
community. There exists a strain toward consistency
(Sumner, 1906, pp. 6, 38 f), between the secondary and
the maintenance mores, the latter exercising a predomin-
ating influence. Also these more abstract systems of
ethics or conduct exert a reciprocal influence and, by
incorporation into the more active or primary phases,
may become more influential in one way or another.
In general, the more removed the mores are from
the preservation of the primary activities of group
life, the more these symbolic standards are supported
merely by group opinion and the like. The closer these
symbolic standards, the mores, are to the material and
economic phases, the greater the amount of physical and
forceful machinery organized to support the mores or
standards in the advent of their failure to function on
their own authority. This is illustrated in political,
diplomatic, legal, and military maintenance of economic
relation. Such control is particularly strong in times of
crisis, when all available means of control are brought into
operation to maintain the established order. The phenomenon of war illustrates such stringent coercive control.
Some symbols are strictly prohibited in speech and press,
while other symbols are especially played up. The
" soldier," the " patriot," the " dollar-a-year men," the
" protection of our homes," " national heroes," are set up
as symbols of emotional unification. National songs,
accompanied by ceremonies, are used as symbols to arouse
group and national spirit and morale. Community song
feasts are organized to arouse spirit for the " cause."
Particularly is the " country's flag " made more actively

a symbolic fetish. Daily ceremonial rites—action—in and out of the soldiery are performed with strict rules and reverence to establish and maintain its symbolic unifying power.

These facts of common experience, which have been analysed by sociological investigators, again emphasize the significance of action in giving content to symbols and in effecting symbolic integration.

In normal times less restriction and more reliance is placed upon symbols themselves to perpetuate and continue existing social organization and customs. It is here that symbols play a particular rôle. They are often fetishes. Almost anything can be done, if smuggled in under the wing of " progress." " Democracy " is a thing to work or fight for. " Success " is a magic word. In order to make symbols more potent, ceremonials—again increase in action content—are carried on in connection with them, such as Spencer, Sumner, Thomas, and many others have described. For instance, in primitive Mexico at the annual festival of the war god, an image of it, made of grain, seeds, and vegetables kneaded with the blood of boys was broken up and " eaten by males only ' after the manner of our communion ' " (Sumner, 1906, p. 337). In modern times, school groups go through ceremonials to establish reverence for " God " and " Country " in preparation for eventual patriotic " sacrifice " if necessary. Ceremonials quite similar to certain primitive rites are practised by some modern religious orders in order to maintain the symbolic prestige of its dogmas regarding personal sacrifice and obligation to other persons and to the god of the group. Symbolic rituals are carried out in founding public institutions, establishing marital relations, or in maintaining legal prestige. Illustrations could be multiplied.

However, due to the fact that group experiences are always different, there is an essential rôle which the symbolic process plays besides merely manipulating such stimuli to which the group must react. The symbolic process is a generalizer of group experience. It thus furnishes a basis for a common understanding and group control.

Symbols integrate the complex social acts of the group; consequently they become functional in co-ordinating group behaviour and effecting a greater division of labour. The systems of sociology which emphasize only similars and like responses have pointed out only one aspect of collective behaviour. Symbolic behaviour gives a constellation, or unification, of the different types of behaviour of the whole social action pattern. Symbols, then, become means of mobilizing and incorporating within themselves dissimilar and varied action content. In addition there is always the fact that the symbol is a group or social affair. The symbol may thus produce concerted group action, although carrying to a remarkable extent different behaviour content due to a division of labour and the co-ordinated activity associated with it. This group control aspect of symbols is so marked that individuals and groups within larger groups at various times act directly counter to their own interests, being subject to the effective influence of group symbols and their reinforcing stimuli.

Some symbols become especially effective as mobilizers of group action. Darkheim, for instance, has emphasized this phase. He has developed the conception of " collective representations," *i.e.*, common social symbols and standards which have developed and live in the life of the group, relatively independent of the sanction of the separate individuals, who are constrained and controlled by them. Lippmann (1922) also, in his stimulating book *Public Opinion*, has analysed the control of stereotype symbols in modern life. These stereotypes are sufficiently vague and general to be influential over a large body of experience, but sufficiently conditioned to action and emotion to be of great effectiveness.

A most significant factor in making effective the control of the group by the use and manipulation of symbols, including the art of propaganda, is the emotional basis and conditioning involved in so many symbols, and particularly those directly bearing upon the more personal integrations affecting the personal " self " and status or existence. These become more capable on that account of being used as control mechanisms. By their use people may be aroused to positive or negative emotional re-actions as was done by the atrocity stories used to work up hatred and fear toward the " Huns." Positive attitudes may also be aroused toward " friends," " brothers " and " pro-tectors." With a strong emotional state the group is then in a position to be influenced by symbols to action in one way or another according to the trend of the aroused emotion and the adroitness with which the emotional drives are directed.

Symbolic integration, as we see, furnishes a remarkable mechanism for the mobilization of group action into a unitary co-ordination. The brain which is a functional part of the symbolic process is admirably constructed to facilitate the domination and utilization of the " vital " or " energetic " reserves of the individuals in group behaviour. In humans, the cerebral mechanisms include highly-specialized secondary associational centres which are free from specific contextual relations and thus are operative as general connections for whatever activity is under way, thus drawing in other behaviour resources. There are nervous elements which are structurally situated so as to function in discharging their vital reserves into whatever associational system is in action. Thus the actions initiated by proper symbolic manipulation may arouse other centres and draw upon the energetic resources of the body in a most effective manner and to a much greater degree, for instance, than is possible among less complexly developed animals (see Herrick, 1926, Ch. XIII and XVII). Although emotions are generally regarded as individual, still the manipulation of symbols which have been properly conditioned to the emotions of the group may thereby produce a group unity and morale which is a powerful means of group control. Such a group morale or emotional group coherence may properly be thought of as a group rather than an individual phenom-enon and may be included under a study of group control.

The mobilization and use of the group's energetic reserves is apt to be an expensive operation, particularly if there is no adequate return for the energy expended. Dodge (1920) has discussed some salient phases of the limits of propaganda, for example. Also, as conditioned responses are an important aspect of both symbolic integration and emotional conditioning, it is important to consider all the limits of such conditioning. To illustrate, Pavlov (1923) has demonstrated the close relation of conditioning to sleep. The dog, for instance, even though very hungry, could be quickly put to sleep by the conditioned stimulus, and even before asleep—while it could still observe meat, it would not make the necessary effort to snatch it. The principles operating here undoubtedly operate in humans as well.

A rational or reflective control of the group to attain a given object or carry out a given programme must take into consideration the above and many other facts regarding social control and group behaviour. The relation of symbols to habitual, so-called rational, emotional, and other forms of individual and group behaviour is, indeed, a fertile field for investigation, but it is outside the scope of the present study to go into an investigation of these mechanisms in detail. This task must await a future effort.

Finally, in regard to the type of social control based upon a rational analysis of facts by those concerned, this is also a special problem for investigation.

Some are of the opinion that groups will never be able to act rationally to any extended degree and that dependence must always be placed upon symbolic control by manipulating customary, irrational, fetish, and emotional modes of group behaviour. Others, however, Veblen for instance, in analysing the effect of modern large-scale, technical machine industry upon reflective behaviour, indicate that people of a necessity will become more causal and logical in their symbolic development. The increasing mechanization of so many phases of life tends to inculcate into behaviour the logic of dependent relationships. Living and particularly occupational work become a matter of the obvious requirement of certain definite acts to produce certain definite results. Automobiles, radio, electricity, machines, are manipulated and operated according to understandable laws. Even present agricultural and domestic economy has lost mystery, it is operated by modern technical devices. Canned corn is an obvious phenomenon. The growing of it may have been a subject of totemic superstition with some Indian tribes, but with modern machinery, irrigation methods, soil culture, and plant breeding there is a mechanical explanation available. This mechanization is carried even to the amusements and leisure activities of the group. Thus not only is the working time spent under these habitual and repeated influences, but it penetrates our whole life. It seems that this inevitably means that control will have to be shifted to a greater and greater dependence upon factual demonstration and to more direct methods of meeting critical or sceptical " show-me " attitudes.

Machine industry and technology does undoubtedly introduce the mass of the population to active participation in causal operations. Their symbolic behaviour must incorporate this type of reflection. The long-run effects are yet to be determined, as well as its relation to rational social control. The symbolic process is obviously in the making.

It is evident that the symbolic process furnishes a most remarkable means of determining group unity, morale, and control. A greater understanding and utilization of its possibilities is undoubtedly a major task in human engineering.

BIBLIOGRAPHY

Alexander (F. M.). 1918: *Man's Supreme Inheritance*. Conscious guidance and control in relation to human evolution in civilization. Introduction by John Dewey.

Allport (F. H.). 1924: *Social Psychology*.

Ament (W.). 1899: *Die Entwicklung von Sprechen und Denken beim Kinde*.

Baldwin (B. T.) and Stecher (Lorle). 1924: *The Psychology of the Pre-school Child*.

Baldwin (J. M.). 1902: *Social and Ethical Interpretations*. Third revised edition.

    1903: "Mind and Body from the Genetic Point of View," *Psychological Review*, **10**: 225–47.

    1906: (a) *Mental Development in the Child and the Race*. Third revised edition.

    1906: (b) *Thought and Things*, Vol. 1.

    1908: *Thought and Things*, Vol. 2.

Barnes (Earl). 1896–7: *A Study in Children's Interests*. Studies in Education. Stanford University. **1**: 203–12.

    1902: *How Words get Content*. Studies in Education. **2**: 41–61.

Bartlett (F. C.) and others. "Is Thinking merely the Action of Language Mechanism?" *British Journal of Psychology*, Vol. XI, pp. 55–104.

Bateman (W. G.). 1914: "A Child's Progress in Speech," *Journal of Educational Psychology*. **5**: 307–21.

    1915: "Two Children's Progress in Speech," *Journal of Educational Psychology*. **6**: 475–93.

    1916: "The Language Status of Three Children at the same Age," *Ped. Sem.* **23**: 211–41.

    1917: *Papers on Language Development*, **24**: 391–8.

Bell (S.). 1903: "The Significance of Activity in Child Life." *Independent*. **4**: 911.

Bernard (L. L.). 1918: Discussion. Papers and Proceedings of American Sociological Society. **12**: 223–8. Ch. U. of C. Press.

    1919–20: The Objective Viewpoint in Sociology. **25**: 298–325.

    1924: *Instinct*: A study in social psychology.

    1926: *An Introduction to Social Psychology*.

Binet (A.). 1890: "Perceptions d'enfant." *Revue Philosophique*. **30**: 582–611.

Blanton (M. G.). 1917: "Behavior of the Human Infant during the First Thirty Days of Life." *Psychological Review*. **24**: 456–83.

Blanton (M. and S.). 1919: *Speech Training in Children*. Century Co.

Block (Oscar). 1923: "Langage d'action dans les premiers stades du langage de l'enfant. *J. de Psychol.* **20**: 670–4.

Bloomfield (Leonard). 1914: *An Introduction to the Study of Language*.

Bogardus (E. S.). 1924 : *Fundamentals of Social Psychology.*
Bohn (W. E.). 1914 : "First Steps in Verbal Expression." *Ped. Sem.* **21** : 578–95.
Bode (Boyd H.) and others. 1917 : *Creative Intelligence.*
Bodenhafer (Walter B.). 1920–1 : "The Comparative Rôle of the Group Concept in Ward's *Dynamic Sociology* and Contemporary American Sociology." *A.J.S.* **26** : 273–314 ; 425–74 ; 588–600 ; 716–43.
Boyd (Wm.). 1914 : "The Development of a Child's Vocabulary." *Ped. Sem.* **21** : 95–124.
Brandenburg (G. C.). 1915 : "The Language of a Three-year-old Child." *Ped. Sem.* **22** : 89–120.
1918 : "Psychological Aspects of Language." *Journal of Educational Psychology.* **9** : 313–32.
Brandenburg (G. C. and J.). 1919 : "Language Development during the Fourth Year. The Conversation." *Ped. Sem.* **26** : 27–40.
Brinton (D. G.). 1890 : *Essays of an Americanist.* Philadelphia.
1892 : "Observations on the Chinantic Language of Mexico." *Proc. American Philos. Soc.* **30** : 22–31.
Also *Studies in South American Native Languages*, pp. 45–105.
Brown (H. C.). 1916 : "Language and the Associative Reflex." *Journal of Phil. Psych. and Sci. Meth.* **13** : 645–9.
Buckman (S. S.). 1897 : "The Speech of Children." *Nineteenth Century.* **16** : 793–807.
Burgess (E. W.). 1923 : "Study of the Delinquent as a Person." *American Journal of Sociology.* **28** : 657–80.
Bühler (Karl). 1922 : *Die geistige Entwicklung des Kindes.* Dritte Auflage.
Bühler (Charlotte). 1927 : *Sociologische und psychologische Studien über das erste Lebensjahr.*
Case (Clarence Marsh). 1923 : *Non-violent Coercion* : a study in methods of social pressure. Century Co. 23.
Cason (Hulsey). 1925 : "General Aspects of Conditioned Response." *Psychological Review,* **32** : 298–316.
1925 : "The Conditioned Reflex or Conditioned Response as a Common Activity of Living Organisms." *Psychol. Bull.* **22** : 445–64.
Chamberlain (A. F.). 1904 : "Child Study and Related Topics in Recent Italian Scientific Literature." *Ped. Sem.,* pp. 508–15.
Chamberlain (A. F. and J. C.). 1904–5 : "Studies of a Child." 1, 2 and 3. *Ped. Sem.* 11–2.
Chamberlain (A. F.). 1906 : *The Child.*
Chamberlain (A. F. and J. C.). 1909 : "Studies of a Child. 'Meanings and definitions in the forty-seventh and forty-eighth months." *Ped. Sem.* **16** : 64–103.
Chambers (W. G.). 1904 : "How Words get Meaning." *Ped. Sem.* **11** : 30–50.
Child (C. M.). 1924 : *Physiological Foundations of Behavior.*
Columbia Associates in Philosophy. 1923 : *An Introduction to Reflective Thinking.*
Compayré (G.). 1896 : *The Intellectual and Moral Development of the Child.* Translated.
Conradi (E.). 1904 : "Psychology and Pathology of Speech Development of the Child." *Ped. Sem.* **11** : 328–80.

Cooley (C. H.). 1902 : *Human Nature and the Social Order.*
    1908 : " A Study of the Early Use of Self-words by a Child." *Psychological Review.* **15** : pp. 339–57.
    1909 : *Social Organization* : a study of the larger mind. New York : Scribner.
    1920 : *Social Process.* New York : Scribner.
    1926 : " The Roots of Social Knowledge." *Amer. J. of Sociology.* **23** : 59–79.
Cushing (F. H.). 1892 : " Manual Concepts : a study of hand-usage on culture-growth." *Amer. Anth.* **5** : 289–318.
Darwin (Charles). 1877 : " A Biographical Sketch of an Infant Mind." **2** : 285–294.
    1878 : *The Descent of Man and Selection in Relation to Sex,* pp. 570–3.
Dashiell (J. F.). 1925 : " A Physiological-behavioristic Description of Thinking." *Psychological Review.* **32** : 54–73.
Deville (Gabriel). 1890–1 : *Notes sur le Développement du Langage. Rev. Ling. et Philol. comp.* 1890 : **23** : 330–43.
    1891 : **24** : 10–42 ; 128–43 ; 242–57 ; 300–20.
Dewey (John). 1894 : " The Psychology of Infant Language." *Psychological Review.* **1** : 63–6.
    1896 : " The Reflex Arc Concept." *Psychological Review.* **3** : 357–70.
    1916 : *Democracy and Education* : an introduction to the philosophy of education.
Dewey (John) and others. 1917 : *Creative Intelligence.*
Dewey, John. 1922 (a) : *Human Nature and Conduct* : an introduction to social psychology.
    1922 (b) : " Knowledge and Speech Reaction." *Journal of Philosophy.* **19** : No. 21 : 561–70. Oct. 12, 1922.
    1925 : *Experience and Nature.*
Dodge (Raymond). 1920 : *The Psychology of Propaganda.* Religious Educ. **15** : 241–52.
Donovan (J.). 1891 : " The Festal Origin of Human Speech." Mind. **16** : 3, pp. 498–506.
Doran (E. W.). 1907 : " A Study of Vocabularies." *Ped. Sem.* **14** : 401–38.
Drevers (J.). 1915 : " A Study of Children's Vocabularies." 1, 2, 3. *Journal of Exp. Ped.* **3** : 34–43 ; 96–102 ; 182–9.
    1919 : " The Vocabulary of a Free Kindergarten Child." *J. Exp. Ped.* **5** : 28–37.
Drummond (M.). 1913 : *The Dawn of Mind.*
Douglass (H. R.). 1925 : " The Development of Number Concepts in Children of Pre-School or Kindergarten Age." *Journal of Exp. Psychol.* **8** : 443–70.
Durkheim (Emile). 1912 : *Le suicide : étude de sociologie.* Deuxième édition.
Ellwood (C. A.). 1912 : *Sociology in its Psychological Aspects.*
    1916–7 : " Objectivism in Sociology." *A.J.S.* **22** : 289–305.
    1918 : *An Introduction to Social Psychology.* New York : Appleton.
    1923–4 : " Scientific Method of Studying Human Society." *J. of S.F.* **2** : 328–32.
    1925 : *The Psychology of Human Society* : an introduction to sociological theory.
Esper (E. A.). 1921 : " The Psychology of Language." *Psychological Bulletin.* **18** : 490–6.

N

Faris (Ellsworth). 1925 (a) : " Pre-literate People : proposing a new term." *A.J.S.* **30** : 710–2.
 1925 (b) : " The Nature of Human Nature." *Papers and Proc. of A.S.S.* **19**.

Follett (M. P.). 1918 : *The New State* : group organization the solution to popular government.

France (Anatole). 1923 : *The Garden of Epicurus.* Translated.

Gale (H. and M. C.). 1900 : " Vocabularies of Three Children of one Family to two and one-half Years of Age." *Psychol. Studies.* **1** : 70–117.

Gale (H.). 1902 : " The Vocabularies of Three Children in one Family at two and three Years of Age." *Ped. Sem.* **9** : 422–35.

Gates (G. S.). 1923 : " An Experimental Study of the Growth of Social Perception." *J. Educ. Psy.* **14** : 449–61.

Gheorgov (J. A.). 1905 : " Die ersten Anfänge des sprachlichen Ausdrucks für das Selbstbewusstsein bei Kindern." *Arch. für die gesammte Psychologie.* **5** : 329–404.

Gesell (A.). 1925 : *The Mental Growth of the Pre-School Child.*

Giddings (F. H.). 1899 : " The Psychology of Society." *Science.* pp. 16–23.
 1918 : " Social Control in a Democracy." *Papers and Proc. of A.S.S.O.* VII. U. of C. Press.
 1920 : *Principles of Sociology : an analysis of the phenomena of association and of social organization.*
 1922 : *Studies in the Theory of Human Society.*

Grant (J. R.). 1915 : " A Child's Vocabulary." *Ped. Sem.* **22** : 183–203.

Guillet (C.). 1917 : " The Growth of a Child's Concepts." *Ped. Sem.* **24** : 81–96.

Hale (H.). 1887 : " The Origin of Language and the Antiquity of Speaking Man." *Trans. Amer. Assn. Adv. of Science.* **35** : 279–323.

Hall (J. W.). 1896–7 : " Five Hundred Days of a Child's Life." *Child Study Mo.* **2** : 330–42 ; 394–407 ; 458–73 ; 522–37 ; 586–608.

Head (Henry). 1920–1 : " Disorders of Symbolic Thinking and Expression." *Brit. J. of Psych.* **11** : 179–93.

Helson (H.). 1925 : " The Psychology of Gestalt." *A.J.P.* **36** : 342–70 ; **37** : 494–526.

Herrick (C. Judson). 1924 : *Neurological Foundations of Animal Behavior.*
 1926 : *Brains of Rats and Men : a survey of the origin and biological significance of the cerebral cortex.*

Hogan (Louise E.). 1898 : *A Study of a Child.*

Heidbreder (Edna). 1924 : *An Experimental Study of Thinking.*

Hollingworth (H. L.). 1926 : *The Psychology of Thought.*

Hollingsworth (Leta S.). 1917 : " Echolia in Idiots : its meaning for modern theories of imitation." *J. of Educ. Psy.* **8** : 212–9.

Horn (M. D.). 1926 : " The Thousand and Three Words most frequently used by Kindergarten Children." *Childhood Education.* pp. 118–22.

Humphrey (G.). 1922–3 : " The Conditioned Reflex and the Elementary Social Reaction." *J.A.P and S.P.* **17** : 113–19.

Hunter (W. S.). 1913–5 : " The Delayed Reaction in Animals and Children." Behavior Monographs. **2** : 5–86.
 1917 : " The Delayed Reaction in a Child." *Psychol. Rev.* **24** : 74–87.

Hunter (W. S.). 1924 : " The Problem of Consciousness." *Psychol. Rev.* **31** : 1–31.
1924 : " The Symbolic Process." *Psychol. Rev.* **31** : 478–97.
Jespersen (Otto). 1923 : *Language : its nature, development, and origin.* Translated.
Jenks (Albert Ernest). 1918 : Discussion. " The ' Half-breed ' Ascendent." *Papers and Proc. of A.S.S.* VII. U. of C. Press.
Kantor (J. R.). 1920 : " Objective Interpretation of Meaning." *A.J. Psy.* **32** : 231–48.
1922 : " An Analysis of Psychological Language Data." *Psychol. Rev.* **29** : 267–309.
Keller (Albert G.). 1916 : *Societal Evolution : a study of the evolutionary basis of the science of society.*
Keller (Helen A.). 1917 : *Story of my Life.*
Kelley (T. L.). 1923 : *Statistical Methods.*
Kelsey (Carl). 1918 : " War as a Crisis in Social Control." *Papers and Proc. of A.S.S.* VII. U. of C. Press.
Kirkpatrick (E. A.). 1891 : " How Children Learn to Talk." *Science.* **18** : 175.
1891 : " Number of Words in an Ordinary Vocabulary." **18** : pp. 107–8.
1919 : *Fundamentals of Child Study.*
Köhler (Wolfgang). 1925 : *The Mentality of Apes.* Translated.
Langenbeck (M.). 1915 : " A Study of a Five-year-old Child." *Ped. Sem.* **22** : 65–88.
Lashley (K. S.). 1920 : " Studies of Cerebral Function in Learning." I : Psychobiology. **2** : 55–135.
1921 (a) : Studies II : " The Effect of Long-continued Practice upon Cerebral Localization." *J. Comp. Psychol.* **1** : 453–68.
1921 (b) : Studies III : " The Motor Areas." *Brain.* **44** : 255–285.
1922 : Studies IV : " Vicarious Function after Destruction of the Visual Area." *Amer. J. of Physiol.* **59** : 44–71. *See also* other studies.
1923 : *The Behavioristic Interpretation of Consciousness.* **30** : 237–72 ; 329–53.
Linder (G.). 1882 : " Beobachtungen und Bermerkungen über die Entwicklung der Sprache des Kindes." *Kosmos,* VI. Jahrgang, XI. Band, pp. 321–42 ; 430–41.
1898 : *Aus dem Naturgarten der Kindersprache.* Leipzig.
Lippmann (W.). 1922 : *Public Opinion.*
Loeb (Jacques). 1925 : *The Mechanistic Conception of Life.*
Lukens (H. L.). 1896 : " Preliminary Reports on the Learning of Language." *Ped. Sem.* **3** : 424–60.
Mach (E.). 1900 : *Language, its Origin, Development and Significance for Scientific Thought.* Open Court. **14** : 171–8.
Magni (J. A.). 1919 : " Vocabularies." *Ped. Sem.* **26** : 209–33.
Malinowski (B.). 1923 : " The Problem of Meaning in Primitive Language," pp. 452–510. Ogden and Richards, *The Meaning of Meaning.*
Major (D. R.). 1906 : *First Steps in Mental Growth.*
Markey (John F.). 1925 : " The Place of Language Habits in a Behavioristic Explanation of Consciousness." *Psychol. Rev.* **32** : 384–401.

Markey (John F.). 1926 : "A Redefinition of Social Phenomena : giving a basis for comparative sociology." *American Journal of Sociology.* **31** : 733–43.

Mateer (F.). 1908 : "The Vocabulary of a Four-year-old Boy." *Ped. Sem.* **15** : 63–74.
    1918 : *Child Behavior.*

Mattson (Marion L.). 1926 : *Unpublished: a study of factors affecting speech activity in a group of nursery school children.*

Mead (George Herbert). 1903 : "Definition of the Psychical." *U. of C. Dec. Pub. Ser.* I, Vol. 3.
    1909 : "Social Psychology as a Counterpart to Physiological Psychology." *Psychol. Bull.* **6**. 12 : 401–8.
    1910 : "What Social Objects must Psychology presuppose ? " *J. of Phil., Psych., and Sci. Methods.* **7** : 174–80.
    1912 : "The Mechanism of Social Consciousness." *J. of Phil.,* etc. **9** : 401–6.
    1913 : "The Social Self." *J. of Phil.,* etc. **10** : 374–80.

Mead (George Herbert) and others. 1917 : *Creative Intelligence.*

Mead (George Herbert). 1922 : "A Behavioristic Account of the Significant Symbol." *J. of Phil.* **19** : 157–63.
    1923 : "Scientific Method and the Moral Sciences." *Internat. Jl. of Ethics.* **33** : 229–47.
    1924–25 : "The Genesis of the Self and Social Control." *Internat. Jl. of Ethics.* **35** : pp. 251–77.

Meumann (E.). 1903 : *Die Sprache des Kindes.*
    1913 : *The Psychology of Learning.*

Mickens (C. W.). 1897 : "Vocabulary." *Child Study Monthly.* **3** : 196–205 ; 260–**269.**

Moore (Mrs. K. C.). 1896 : "Mental Development of a Child." *Monog. Supp. to Psychol. Rev.* **1** : 3.

Mott (A. J.). 1900 : *The Ninth Year of a Deaf Child's Life.* U. of Minn.

Moyer (H. B.). 1911 : *Speech Development.* Monograph U. of Pa. Studies.

Müller (Max). 1870 : *Lectures on the Science of Language.* 1st Series.
    1887 : *Science of Thought.*

Nice (M. M.). 1915 : "The Development of a Child's Vocabulary in Relation to the Environment." *Ped. Sem.* **22** : 35–64.
    1917 : "Speech Development of a Child from Eighteen Months to Six Years." *Ped. Sem.* **24** : 204–24.
    1918 : "Ambidexterity and Delayed Speech-development." *Ped. Sem.* **25** : 141–162.
    1919 : "A Child's Imagination." *Ped. Sem.* **26** 173–201.
    1920 : "Concerning All-day Conversations." *Ped. Sem.* **27** : 166–77.
    1925 : "A Child who would not Talk." *Ped. Sem.* **32** : 105–142.

Northcott (Clarence H.). 1918–9 : "The Sociological Theories of Franklin H. Giddings." *A.J.S.* **24** : 1–23.

Ogburn, (W. F.). 1922 : *Social Change.*

Ogden (C. K.) and Richards (I. A.). 1923 : *The Meaning of Meaning : a study of the influences of language upon thought and of the science of symbolism.*

Ogden (C. K.). 1926 : *The Meaning of Psychology.*

O'Shea (M. V.). 1907 : *Linguistic Development and Education.*

Ouspensky (P. D.). 1922 : *Tertium Organum.*

Park and Burgess. 1924 : *Introduction to the Science of Sociology.*

Pavlov (I. P.). 1923 : " The Identity of Inhibition with Sleep and Hypnosis." *Scientific Monthly.* **17** : 603–8.
Pelsma (J.). 1910 : " A Child's Vocabulary and its Development." *Ped. Sem.* **17** : 328–69.
Pearson (Ruth). 1926 : *The Behavior of the Pre-school Child.* **31** : 800–11.
Perez (B.). 1887 : *The First Three Years of Childhood.* Translated. 2nd edition.
Peterson (J.). 1924 : " Intelligence conceived as a Mechanism." *Psychol. Rev.* **31** : 281–7.
Piaget (Jean). 1926 : *The Language and Thought of the Child.* Translated.
Preyer (W.). 1892 : *The Mind of the Child.*
Rasmussen (Wilhelm). 1920 : *Child's Psychological Development in the First Four Years.*
Romanes (G. J.). 1889 : *Mental Evolution in Man,* Ch. 5–9, 12, 13, 17.
Ross (E. A.). 1909 : " What is Social Psychology ? " *Psychol. Bull.* **6,** 409–11.
    1919 (a) : *Foundations of Sociology,* 5th ed.
    1919 (b) : *Social Psychology.*
    1920 (a) : *Social Control :* a survey of the foundations of order.
    1920 (b) : *Principles of Sociology.*
Rowe (E. C. and H. H.). 1913 : " The Vocabulary of a Child at Four and Six." *Ped. Sem.* **20** : 187–208.
Rugg (H. O.). 1917 : *Statistical Methods applied to Education.*
Sapir (E.). 1921 : *Language : an introduction to the study of speech.*
Schäfer (Paul). 1921 : " Die kindliche Entwicklungsperiode des reinen Sprachverständnisses nach ihrer Abgrenzung." **22** : 317–25. *Zeitsch. für päd. Psychol.*
Seago (Dorothy W.). 1925 : *An Analysis of Language Factors in Intelligence Tests.* Mental Measurement Monographs, Series 1.
Semon (R. W.). 1921 : *The Mneme.* Translated.
Shaw (E. R.). 1896 : " A Comparative Study in Children's Interests." *Child Study Monthly,* July and Aug. pp. 152–67.
Sherrington (C. S.). 1906 : *The Integrative Action of the Nervous System.*
Shinn (M. W.). 1893 and 1907 : " Notes on the Development of a Child." U. of Calif. Pub. Educ. Vol. 1 and 4.
Singer (E. A.). 1924 : *Mind as Behavior and Studies in Empirical Idealism.*
Small (Maurice H.). 1900 : " On some Psychical Relations of Society and Solitude." *Ped. Sem.* **7** : 32–36.
Smith (Madorah). 1925 : *The Development of Vocabulary and Sentence-structure in Pre-school Children.*
Smith and Guthrie. 1921 : *General Psychology in Terms of Behavior.*
Spencer (Herbert). 1893 : *The Principles of Sociology,* Vol. II.
Stern (Frau Clara, and William). 1907 : *Die Kindersprache.* Leipzig.
Stern (W.). 1924 : *Psychology of Early Childhood.*
Sweet (Henry). 1909 : *The History of Language.*
Sully (J.). 1903 : *Studies of Childhood.*
Sumner (W. G.). 1906 : *Folkways.*
Taine. 1877 : " On the Acquisition of Language by Children." *Mind.* **2** : 252–9.
Tanner (A. E.). *The Child.*
Terman (L. M.) and Childs (H. G.). 1912 : " A Tentative Revision and Extension of the Binet-Simon Measuring Scale of Intelligence." *J. Educ. Psy.* **3** : 61–74 ; 133–43 ; 198–208 ; 277–89.

Terman (L. M.). 1918 : "The Vocabulary Test as a Measure of Intelligence." *J. Educ. Psy.* **9** : 452–66.
 1919 : "Some Data on the Binet Test of Naming Words." *J. of Educ. Psy.* **10** : 29–35.

Thomas (William I.). 1909 : *Source Book for Social Origin.* 4th edition.

Thomas (William I.) and Znaniecki. 1920 : *The Polish Peasant in Europe and America.* Vols. i–iv.

Thorndike (Edward L.). 1920 : *Educational Psychology.* Vol. 1 : The Original Nature of Man.

Thorson, H. M. 1925 : "The Relation of Tongue Movements to Internal Speech." *J. Exper. Psychol.* **8** 1–32.

Thurstone (L. L.). 1923 : "The Stimulus Response Fallacy in Psychology." *Psychol. Rev.* **30** : 354–69.

Tracy (F.). 1909 : *The Psychology of Childhood.*

Trettien (A. W.). 1904 : "The Psychology of the Language Interest in Children." *Ped. Sem.* **11** : 113–77.

Veblen, Thorstein. 1917 : An Inquiry into the Nature of Peace and the Terms of Its Perpetuation.

Vendryes (J.). 1925 : *Language : a linguistic introduction to history.* Translated.

Walton (A. C.). 1915 : "The Influence of Diverting Stimuli during Delayed Reaction in Dogs." *J. Anim. Behav.* **5** : 259–91.

Ward (L. F.). 1893 : *The Psychic Factors of Civilization.*
 1898 (a) : *Outlines of Sociology.*
 1898 (b) : "The Essential Nature of Religion." *Inter. J. of Ethics.* **8** : 169–192.
 1906 : *Applied Sociology : a treatise on the conscious improvement of society by society.*
 1910 : *Dynamic Sociology,* Vols. i–ii.
 1911 : *Pure Sociology.*

Watson (John B.). 1914 : *Behavior : an introduction to comparative psychology.*
 1924 : *Psychology from the Standpoint of a Behaviorist.*
 1925 : *Behaviorism.* The People's Institute Pub. Co., N.Y.

Weiss (A. P.). 1918 : "Conscious Behavior." *J. of Phil., Psy., and Sci. Methods.* **15** : 631–41.
 1922 : "Behavior and the Central Nervous System." *Psychol. Rev.* **29** : 329–43.
 1924 : "Biophysical and Biosocial Equivalents in Human Behavior." *Psychol. Bull.* **21** : 86–9.
 1924 : "Behaviorism and Behavior." *Psychol. Rev.* **31** : 32–50 ; 118–49.
 1925 : *A Theoretical Basis of Human Behavior.*

Whipple (G. M.). 1908 : *Vocabulary and Word-Building Tests.*

Whitney (W. D.). 1892 : *Max Müller and the Science of Language.*
 1916 : *The Life and Growth of Language.*

Wolff (Fanny E.). 1897 : "A Boy's Dictionary." *Child Study Monthly.* **3** : 141–50.

Woodworth (R. S.). 1924 : "Four Varieties of Behaviorism and the Lack of Inherent Connection between them." Programme of Amer. Psychol. Assn. *Psychol. Bull.* **21** : p. 89.

Wundt (W.). 1916 : *Elements of Folk Psychology.* Translated. Ch. i.

Yerkes (R. M.). 1916 : *The Mental Life of Monkeys and Apes : a study of ideational behavior.* Behavior Monograph. **3.** 156 pp.
 1925 : *Almost Human.*

Yule (G. U.). 1912 : *Introduction to the Theory of Statistics.*

INDEX

CPSIA information can be obtained at www.ICGtesting.com
Printed in the USA
LVOW130259220612

286906LV00004B/121/P

9 781163 148983